THE
*LACY TECHNIQUES*
OF
*SALESMANSHIP*

# THE
# LACY TECHNIQUES
## OF
# SALESMANSHIP

## PAUL J. MICALI
President of Lacy Sales Institute, Inc.

HAWTHORN BOOKS, INC.
*Publishers*
NEW YORK

*To Doris*

# PREFACE

$S$alesmanship, like everything else, has a style. Aside from the fact that no two people sell in the very same way, people who are formally trained in selling methods will acquire a style. It is usually a better and, therefore, much more effective one than that they developed on their own.

After reading this book and digesting its contents the reader, if he perfects the suggested selling techniques, will be in a position to adopt a style of salesmanship which originated with Jack Lacy in 1938; since, adaptations have been made, up-dating his basic techniques to favorably influence today's buyer. Even though refined over and over again, the original specific goals of simplicity and impact have always been kept in mind. Over 1 million salesmen have been exposed to the Lacy selling techniques. Comments have always been favorable. Some of our most distinguished business leaders are disciples of the Lacy selling philosophy. Here is what a few of them have said:

"Salesmanship as practiced and taught by Lacy is deceptively simple yet most practical and effective. It works."
> GRAYDON L. WALKER
> *Vice President, Parke Davis & Co.*

"His ability to simplify selling techniques so that anyone could understand and use them was outstanding."
> ARTHUR H. "RED" MOTLEY
> President, *Parade* Magazine
> Former Chairman, U.S. Chamber of Commerce

"At a time when the trend was to surround sales training with scientific hocus pocus, Lacy reduced it to simple fundamentals that anyone could learn."

HARRY R. WHITE
Executive Director
Sales Executives Club of New York

"Have used the sales materials produced by Lacy for many years, over and over again, and it has been extremely helpful not only with new men but with veterans as well."

LARRY E. DOYLE
President, Forest Lawn Memorial Parks
Former President, Sales and Marketing Executives—International

"While selling in today's market place is becoming increasingly complex, Lacy understood the fundamentals which have remained the same. He recognized selling as a service."

T. VINCENT LEARSON
President, IBM

If you accept the words of these successful businessmen and if you are willing to deal with the subject of salesmanship with a very open mind, you have a tremendous treat in store for you.

# CONTENTS

# INTRODUCTION

*E*veryone who is connected with selling in any way considers himself a good salesman. This is a general statement, to say the least, but the world is filled with generalities— and this is one of the most prevalent. What's worse, it comes awfully close to the truth.

Let a man be at the right place at the right time with the right product under the right circumstances and he'll tell you what a great selling job he did. The very same man, however, never tells you how many sales he's lost. Is it ego? Is it an occupational hazard? Is it positive thinking as opposed to negative thinking? Whatever it is, there is little question that this trait can be found in almost any salesman, in any industry, in every town

It's a serious matter. Much more serious than people realize. Serious because the large number of salesmen who have this attitude rarely look for ways and means through which to become better salesmen. They don't believe that this type of knowledge can be derived from books, or courses, or films, or any such. Worse yet, they don't really believe that a salesman can become a *professional* salesman. How wrong they are. Rejoice that *you* are not among them.

Our present economy is such that the selling function is more important than ever. However, it must be performed on a much higher plane than ever before. The business world is more complicated. The computer has interjected a swiftness into business which is almost terrifying. The sales prospect, although still human, is more sophisticated. More and more frequently he is college trained. He reads more, he knows more, he is kept abreast of competition by astute competitors and is made even sharper during his relaxing hours through the medium of television and other diversional activities. To sell him isn't easy any more. He no longer responds to the slap on the back or the funny story. He may respond, but *not* with an order. He wants to be sold professionally. He wants to be convinced that he is buying the right product, in the right quantity, at the right time, from the right salesman and the right company.

Therefore, the salesman of today has to react and interact in many different ways to many different people. In addition to knowing his product thoroughly—regardless of how technical it may be—he has to be a psychologist with one prospect, a human computer with another, an adviser with still another, and at the same time a friend with a few buyers in some areas. While he may, and should, show respect for himself, he must never be egotistical to any degree. He must adjust his own personality on every call, making sure that what he says and does is compatible with the personality of each prospect. When objections come up, and they usually do, he must remember and practice the cardinal rule of always giving the prospect a decent respect for his opinion. Then he can proceed to try to change the prospect's thinking.

In the course of the interview he may be asked questions about packaging, merchandising, tolerances, dependability, fair trade laws, availability, freight schedules, warehousing, advertising, quantity prices, credit, contracts, specifications, trends, etc., etc. Of course, he can occasionally say, "I really don't know but I will find out for you," but today this "out" can't be used very often with very many prospects. He is *expected* to know. The prospect usually gives the order only to the salesman in whom he has confidence. That confidence is built up in the course of an interview or in some cases a series of interviews. It's built up by knowing answers to the questions that are being posed.

However, one should never conclude that becoming a walking encyclopedia brings success in selling. To know as many answers as possible is important, but to know how to present one's product or service is even more important. Understanding salesmanship thoroughly is an undertaking with which not enough people have bothered. Yet to practice good, sound, time-tested selling techniques requires a complete understanding of what actually happens during each face-to-face interview on every sales call.

To get the most out of this book the reader should adopt the attitude that there is a great deal more to selling than what meets the eye. That every single step of a sales call should be thoroughly thought out and prepared for, and the selected techniques practiced until they are perfected. There are many ways in which the salesman can be much more effective with the very same product and, sometimes, with the very same statements. That to be thoroughly organized, saleswise, means making a presentation using a logical pattern, as well as being able to assess the response by knowing when it's time to close, how to close, and so on.

It behooves all of us in selling to constantly search for new and better ways to produce the sales on which our economy depends. Much like the doctor, the dentist, the lawyer, or the aeronautical engineer—today's salesman must keep himself thoroughly informed on the latest techniques employed in his profession. If you accept this viewpoint and if you apply the contents of the following chapters to your daily activities, one thing is certain: this book will *significantly change your life*—for the better.

# THE
# LACY TECHNIQUES
# OF
# SALESMANSHIP

# THE ROADMAP TO RICHES IN SELLING

*Let's* start with the basic premise that unless you understand what you're doing you'll never do it well. This certainly applies to salesmanship as well as anything else. Yet strange as it may seem, there are thousands of salesmen who really don't understand what they're doing, how they're doing it and in some instances why they're doing it. Maybe it's because selling comes naturally to some people. I use the word "some" loosely for the ones to whom it comes naturally are in the definite minority. Most people have to work at it. In so doing, they find it difficult to really understand what it's all about.

1

Practically all of us learn to sell in the very same way. We get as much information as we can about a proposition and we begin making sales calls. It becomes a hit and miss situation. We try everything we can possibly think of, adopting the things that work and discarding the ones that fail.

### Acquiring the basic 3 C's

At first, nothing seems to work. We take a mental beating wherever we go. But our determination drives us into making call after call. It's most discouraging. There are times that we decide that we would rather be doing anything else but making calls. But we go on making them.

At this point the salesman who will succeed possesses one important and outstanding qualification—*courage*. This is the quality that will not allow him to give up—and because he will not give up, sooner or later he will make his first sale. What made the difference? At this point he honestly may not know—but he must assume that somehow he has said the right thing at the right time—and he will try to continue this pattern. Inevitably succeeding calls will produce more sales and the salesman acquires a second quality—that of *conquest*. Now it is easier to keep on going. The salesman becomes more satisfied with his work as he becomes more successful. Suddenly, out of thin air, a new quality has developed. The salesman has achieved *confidence*. No salesman can succeed without it. Courage, conquest, confidence, these 3 C's are basic requirements for the beginning salesman.

Having tasted success, the salesman is more free to observe other salesmen—and to discover that though he has been successful there are others who are more successful. On occasion he finds one who is a human dynamo. It seems that every time this man speaks he makes a sale. Ob-

viously, there must be something different about him—
and there is. Statistics have shown, over and over again,
that in any company employing 100 salesmen or more,
approximately 75 percent of the sales are brought in by
only 25 percent of the salesmen. Think of it. One fourth of
the sales staff is bringing in three fourths of the sales! This
makes each man in the top quarter nine times more effective than those in the remaining three quarters.

How can one man outsell another nine-fold? When we
get the answer we will know what it is that makes star salesmen. To do so we must start at the very beginning and
determine what enables a man to achieve success in sales
work. Three elements are involved:

*1. You must master your product or service.*

You must know everything about it, what it does and
how it is made. You must know the competitive conditions
of your industry thoroughly. You must also know what
your competitor is saying about his product as well as what
he is saying about your product. All of this is called *technical knowledge.*

*2. You must be willing to work as hard as you
possibly can.*

If you are spending an average of 4 hours a day on territory and suddenly you should decide that you will work 8
hours each day, you will at least *double* your sales. That is
a mathematical certainty simply because you have twice
as many opportunities of making a sale and also because
you are gaining "steam" as the day progresses.

*3. You must develop a sales personality.*

No matter how much technical knowledge you *may*
possess nor how many hours you are willing to work, your
efforts are almost wasted if your personality is not sales

oriented. The quality of your salesmanship is directly proportionate to the kind of effect that you produce on others through your personality.

Still another very important factor in developing your maximum selling skill is the ability to transmit your feelings to others. Many call this enthusiasm, but it is one thing to be enthusiastic about your product and something else to be able to transmit your enthusiasm to the people you hope to convince. To transmit enthusiasm you must have a feel for the far-reaching process known as timing. In sales work timing consists of the ability to give simultaneous expression to your thoughts through your words, your voice, and your actions. It is quite possible to give one impression with your words, still another with your voice, and a third with your actions. If you do this simultaneously, your timing is off and you don't score with your prospect. But when your words, voice, and actions all give the same impression at the same time, your timing is perfect and you develop tremendous selling power. In an effort to master timing one should develop a natural rhythm of modulation and accentuation coupled with a change of pace. With such a formula you can bring your full powers of impressiveness and persuasiveness into instinctive action without any conscious effort on your part. While timing may sound difficult it really is not. Devote a modest amount of consistent thought and practice to it and in a relatively short period of time it becomes practically automatic.

However, at such a point in your early selling career, when the 3 C's, your enthusiasm, and your timing seem to provide you with a modest amount of success, you must be very careful. This is a very critical point because far too many salesmen assume that now they know what selling is all about. Little do they realize that they have only scratched the surface. There is so much more to making a sale that the average salesman finds it hard to comprehend. Those who dig in deeper, never quenching their thirst for more selling knowledge, go on to become extremely successful. Those who become self-satisfied become stagnant and, worse still, they refuse to blame themselves for it. The cause is always attributed to the product, the service, the territory, the economy, or other outside factors.

The most complicated activity in existence could very well be the art or science of selling. Some argue that it is definitely an art, while others insist that it is a science. It really doesn't matter in which category you place it. The subject is a complicated one—so complicated that people have gone through an entire lifetime without coming close to figuring it out. Why is it so complicated? To begin with, because it is so psychological; it has so many variables; and, it is so difficult to stereotype. No two people buy a particular product or service for the same reason. Not all sales can be closed in the same fashion. Not all territories (or industries or individuals), will resuond to the same tactics. The influencing factors are endless.

When all is said and done, the key point in making a sale has been reached when the salesman has said the right *thing* at the right *time* in the right *way*. It may sound easy but those with real selling experience know that it certainly is not.

### Recognizing the three types of sales

In order to develop the delicate skill of professional salesmanship one must first realize that there are three types of sales. At least he then knows in which ball park he is playing. First there is the *service sale*. This is the type of sale that is usually made in retailing. You probably recall the last time that you walked into a department store to purchase a new tie. After deciding which one you really wanted you gave it to the sales person who accepted your money, wrote out a sales slip, placed the tie in a bag and handed it to you thereby consummating the transaction. If you were lucky, you got a "thank you." The amount of selling involved was really negligible. You made all the decisions on your own. The sales person merely rendered a little service. So little, that in a self-service store such a sales person is completely eliminated. The cashier checks you out on leaving. You bought. No one sold you.

Secondly, there is the *negotiation sale*. This is the type of sale when you also make most of the decisions on your own but the sales person upgrades you a little. For example, you drive into a gasoline station for the purpose of purchasing snow tires for your car. After selecting the tires and discussing the price, the service-station attendant convinces you that for only a few dollars more you could have snow tires with white walls. They will match the front tires (which are white-walled) and the car will look better. Here there is a little negotiating involved but not too much selling. You had decided initially that you wanted and needed the snow tires. You drove in with the definite intention of buying.

The third type of sale is called the *creative sale*. To create a sale means to bring it into existence. It means that you create a need in the mind of the prospect for a product or service which he didn't realize he could use. This is the best type of sale for it not only does most for our economy but it also brings the best rewards to the salesman. Here is where real salesmanship is involved. Invariably, the salesmen who earn the largest sums of money are those involved in creative selling. Therefore this book will, for the most part, concern itself with creative selling—for obviously the greatest amount of selling skill is necessary in creating a sale where there might not ordinarily have been one.

### Developing Creativity

How do you develop selling skill? I wish there were a specific answer. Obviously there isn't. Beware of the person who tells you that he can make you a *super*-salesman overnight—doubling or even tripling your sales in the process. (The last plausible definition I heard of a *super*-salesman:—"an s.o.b. from the home office with a special price.") You *can* become a *super*-salesman in terms of success—but it won't be overnight and it takes a big effort on your part. So big, that not too many people make it. That's why a yearly U.S. analysis of salesmen's income repeatedly shows that a large number of them (about 25 percent) do little more than earn a decent living. Another 20 percent have an income which is substantially above average. And, only about 5 percent earn fantastic sums of money—year after year.

What makes the big difference? Why are the very successful so few in number? People are people. We are all endowed with a brain, a voice and legs to take us to the prospect. Where is the dividing line and why? Well, to claim to have the answer is ridiculous. Nobody has the *complete* answer. We wonder if anybody ever will have it. But, let's examine what seems to bring about success in selling. If you can pinpoint why one person succeeds, you will have discovered a good part of the answer.

There are three things in the mind of a salesman which determine how successful he will be in selling:

1. Will Power    2. Memory    3. Imagination

No need to spend any time discussing *will power*. It's a

fundamental virtue possessed by most of us in varying degrees. We can assume that you have an abundance of will power. If you didn't, you wouldn't get out of bed in the morning and make the day a productive one. If you didn't have will power, you wouldn't be reading this book. *Memory,* too, is something we need not ponder over. Once you have learned what your proposition is all about you certainly don't have trouble remembering what to say when you're face to face with the prospect. Especially since you say almost the very same things over and over again on every sales call. *Imagination,* however, must be discussed, most thoroughly. *It is the key to success in selling.* You will never reach your full potential in selling until you have learned to develop and use your selling imagination. You've heard a great deal said about imagination— the term has been bandied about in many a sales meeting or sales seminar. You probably have said to yourself, many times, that you agree that imagination is necessary in selling. But—most likely—you left it at that. You didn't ask yourself, "Can I use more imagination in my daily selling activities?" Well, you can and you must—if you want to achieve limitless success in selling. You can start doing so right now. You need simply change the way in which you present your product or service. Not a big change . . . but a most significant one.

Your statements about the many merits of your proposition will remain the same—but you will begin to apply imagination. To accomplish this you must do one very important thing. Find out:

1. What is the prospect's dominant desire?
2. What is he trying to do?
3. What does *he* want most?

*Then build your presentation around it.* The prospect's dominant desire is his *Hot Button.* And the more often that you can hit it during your presentation, the greater are your chances of making the sale. It's a gimicky phrase —*Hot Button*—and it's meant to be so that you won't forget it. This phrase is so important that we copyrighted it years ago. Hot Button salesmanship is so important that it can *change your life*—can mean the difference between an average income and a very substantial one.

### Using the Hot Button technique

The Hot Button method is not difficult to use—in fact, it's really quite easy. What *is* hard is remembering to use it. If you are among the nearly 90 percent of salesmen who automatically give the prospect a "full dose" on every call —you have developed the habit of doing most of the talking during a sales presentation. You tell him *all* of the features and *all* of the benefits of your product or service and you go on and on. (Some people are in love with the sound of their own voice.) The prospect listens because he's polite. But with only one ear—and usually, with a bored expression on his face. At the very end of your monologue you try to close him, he comes up with some reason why he can't or won't buy and then you leave thanking him for his time. Sounds silly, doesn't it? But this is the way that most salesmen sell. They could just as well open the interview by saying: "Look, Mr. Prospect—I'm here to tell you my story and, as I fly along, if you figure out how you can use what I'm selling—stop me and we'll do business." He doesn't stop the fast talker—and they don't do business.

A much more sensible (and more effective) way of selling is the Hot Button way. It capitalizes on a specific aspect of normal human behavior. Psychologists have proved that *94 percent of the time people are thinking about themselves*. Hard to believe, isn't it? But it's true. You can prove it to yourself very easily. From now on, when you're engaged in conversation with *anyone,* listen carefully and categorize the subject matter. You'll find that the other person is talking about himself almost constantly. It's always been so—but you probably never paid too much attention to this human tendency.

Maybe something like this will sound familiar. You're walking down main street in your home town and you meet Jack, whom you haven't seen for a few months. You're glad to see him. So you say, "Hi, Jack, how are you?" He says, "I'm fine, *now.*" And you make the mistake of asking, "Why Jack, have you been sick?" And he's off. A twenty-minute dissertation on his operation. All the gory details. His long hospital stay, his gas pains, his intravenous feedings, his bout with death, etc., etc. Only because you're on a public street does he refrain from pulling down his pants and showing you his scar.* At the end of all this, if you're *lucky,* he might say, "and how have *you* been?" But generally, you're not that lucky. By this time *he* realizes that *he* has spent too much of *his* time talking with you and *he* now is late for *his* appointment with *his* optician to pick up *his* bifocals so *he* can read the feature story about *his* company carrying *his* photograph in *his* newspaper with *his* breakfast without straining *his* eyes.

So, you see, this preoccupation with one's own problems (or dominant desires), is something to be completely aware of at all times. To capitalize on it is by no means sinful. It's simply a way of getting through to people using language to which they will be sensitive and to which they will quickly respond.

---

* Some people, however, will do it anyway. You will recall that a modern-day U.S. president was asked about his operation during a press conference. He not only went into the details but exposed his scar— and a picture of it appeared on the front pages of newspapers across the country.

Some salesmen seem to be born with the instinctive ability to zero in on the dominant desires or Hot Buttons of others. Most, however, have to work hard at developing this technique. And a certain number go through an entire lifetime without ever latching on to the idea—having thereby placed a constant ceiling on their earning power.

I shall never forget an instinctive display of Hot Button selling which I once witnessed. It happened some time ago —during World War II.

I was a naval officer stationed in Hawaii and fortunate enough to be there for an entire year. Every Sunday my friends and I would go to church in Honolulu. They would routinely march down the aisle, sit down front and take everything in. I would sit in the rear. Mainly because, at the conclusion of the services, I would be among the first to leave. I could then enjoy that glorious Hawaiian climate as I waited for my friends. One Sunday morning I was waiting on the sidewalk as usual and I noticed a boy, about fourteen, running up and down the front steps of the church selling orchids to the people as they came out. Now, there's nothing unusual about an orchid in Hawaii because they are so plentiful. They practically grow wild along the sides of the highways. You could buy them, then, in any flower shop for fifty cents. But this kid was selling them for a dollar. But what's more important—he was selling three out of every four people he approached. (You'd settle for that selling ratio right now, wouldn't you? make four calls—and get three orders.) And I was going crazy trying to figure out what it was that he said to make him so effective.

When the crowd thinned out, and my friends finally appeared, I said to the boy, "Son, can I see you for a minute?" He rushed over and said, "Orchid, sir?"

"Not really, I just want to ask you a question."

"Yes, sir." (He was most polite.)

"You know," I said, "I've been watching you closely and I noticed that you sold about three out of every four people you approached."

"That's right, sir."

"Well, tell me, what do you say that makes them buy?"

A big smile came over his face as he said, "You see, sir, it's like this. I only approach couples, and before I say anything I look at the lady's left hand. If she's wearing a wedding ring, I say, '*Miss,* wouldn't you like to have your boyfriend buy you an orchid?' If she isn't wearing a wedding ring, then I approach the man and I say, 'Sir, how about buying your *wife* an orchid.' "

At the tender age of fourteen this kid had figured out that those who are married would rather not be—and vice versa. (It took me years to find that out.)

But do you see how quickly he was able to get through to people and hit a common, prevalent Hot Button? In so doing—he was able to not only maintain an extremely high ratio of closes but also sell a product at twice the going price.

Anyone can become that effective in selling provided that he wants to adopt, and constantly use, the Hot Button method. And don't begin to rationalize as to why it won't work for you in your industry or with your product or service. It will, if you try and keep on trying! The most common rationalization is centered around the argument that you can't very well use Hot Button salesmanship on a prospect if you can't find out what his Hot Button is. Agreed. But whose fault is that? If you let the prospect talk—early in the interview—you'll be surprised at how quickly Hot Buttons begin to spurt out of his mouth. Ninety-four per cent of the time—remember? In a matter of minutes he'll start telling you his problems, his likes, his dislikes, his needs—all of them loaded with possible Hot Buttons just waiting for the right salesman to press them.

And even if he doesn't seem to want to talk—you still can find out what his Hot Button may be. Just ask a few questions. No harm in this. Very few will refuse to answer. But you must remember to force yourself to ask. Example:

Dick and Lucille, dear friends of ours for some twenty years, moved from one part of the country to another about every two or three years. As a promising executive of a large insurance company, Dick would get periodic promotions and each time it meant relocation. The process of effecting each move had a repetitive pattern. Dick would go on to his new assignment leaving Lucille behind to sell their house. Once it was sold she would join Dick in a motel in the new city, contact local realtors and go out with them to look at available houses.

A tender, quiet individual, Lucille was not a great conversationalist with real estate brokers she'd be meeting for the first time. In fact, she had to be asked a question for her to speak. As houses were routinely shown to her, she would routinely turn them down with a minimum of conversation. She was particularly proud of one special piece of furniture they owned,—an unusually large breakfront. Not too many houses would have a windowless wall large enough to accommodate it. So when Lucille stepped into a house—she had only one thought in mind. Is there a wall in the dining room or living room large enough for my breakfront? (This was her constant Hot Button.) If there wasn't, the house was automatically unacceptable. The brokers never asked why—and she never volunteered the information. Finally, when she happened to enter *the* house with *the* appropriate wall, the problem would be solved. She'd summon Dick and they'd buy the house.

This happened every time Dick got transferred and Lucille went house hunting. The dozens of real estate brokers she worked with—in several states—all missed the boat. *Not one* asked her the simple question—"what type of house would you like to have?" or "what are your needs?" Had they been sharp enough to ask,—they would have learned her Hot Button at the very outset, saved loads of time and made an easy sale.

If the prospect is allowed to talk, he will usually tell you his dominant desire—around which you should build your presentation. If he doesn't tell you—then by all means ask a few questions which will steer him into telling you.

Incidentally, unlike Lucille, the average prospect does not always have one Hot Button. Or the same one on each interview. On one call you'll find that his dominant desire is more profit. On another it's quality, or more sales, or convenience, etc., etc. The idea is to zero in on the Hot Button of the moment and press it as often as you can throughout the sales call.

Maybe you think this whole approach to selling is not for you. It is quite possible that you might regard it as a way of taking unfair advantage of a prospect. Forget it. You'll find that the prospect never reacts unfavorably. Why would he? Whenever you've been approachd by a salesman who quickly told you what was in it for you, didn't you feel that he handled you well? And, if in so doing he continually referred to your dominant desire— you didn't mind, did you? After all, he was interested in *you* and talked about *you* throughout the interview.

Make a promise to yourself, right now, that you will begin to use Hot Button salesmanship on your very next sales call. It will literally change your life. And the pros-

pect will be very happy with you. Why? Read the following
—it's called "The Prospect's Prayer."

## PROSPECT'S PRAYER

When you come in to call on me,
    I'm as busy as a man can be.
I'm thinking of the things that do
    The most to bring more business through.

I care not what your name may be,
    Nor who sent you to call on me.
I want to know what I may win
    If I should stop to let you chin.

You won't get long to sing your song
    So, make your presentation strong.
Don't tell me your company's history,
    Just tell what you can do for me.

Remember, sir, you came to sell
    And not a lengthy tale to tell.
And you won't sell me by boastful struttin',
    You'll do it only by hitting my HOT BUTTON.*

* Copyright 1961, Lacy Sales Institute, Inc. Used by permission.

# DEVELOPING A WINNING SALES PERSONALITY

*There* are some things that must always come first. When building a house one must first start with a foundation. Then he can build a structure upon it which will stand firm and won't topple over.

In the constant process of self improvement the salesman should build on a foundation too. That foundation is his personality. He must build it solidly or success is simply

17

unattainable. All of the greatest selling techniques in the world will be useless to him if his personality is not able to come into play as necessary in the process of making a sale. As marketing management people know—a good product placed in the hands of a weak salesman won't sell. Yet, place a fair product in the hands of a strong salesman —and he'll break all records. His strength, for the most part, is due to his personality.

When was the last time that you gave very much thought to the subject of personality? Specifically—*your* personality. Most of us give it only a fleeting thought on rare occasions. Our ego tells us that we have a great personality— and we accept this—easily and happily. A mistake—to be sure. The subject of personality is a critical one—and it deserves early attention in any book of this type.

## This thing called personality

"When you were born you broke the mold." This expression has been used in jest for generations but it contains more truth than humor. No two of us are alike— particularly when it comes to personality. Oh, I know, most of us who sell think we're dynamic. But what does the prospect or customer really think?

What *is* personality? Ever try to define it? Just think about it for 30 seconds. . . . Not easy, is it? Don't feel badly, though, because even Webster had trouble. After years of thinking about it (and training salesmen) we've come up with this definition: "Personality is a mental or psychic atmosphere that we radiate about ourselves which determines the impression we produce on others." It's everything we are, everything we do. The way we look, act, speak, dress, smile, react, respond—the list is endless.

The attributes of which a personality may be comprised

run into hundreds. The combinations in which these attributes reveal themselves in different personalities are countless. A discussion of this subject is overwhelming; its enormity and importance is staggering.

We can begin to comprehend the tremendous scope of the subject when we list a few of the desirable attributes of a sales personality:

| | |
|---|---|
| Courage | Persistence |
| Tolerance | Intelligence |
| Imagination | Refinement |
| Frankness | Poise |
| Humility | Initiative |
| Sincerity | Foresight |
| Honesty | Logic |
| Culture | Enthusiasm |
| Originality | Concentration |
| | |
| Energy | Contancy |
| Industry | Self-control |
| Generosity | Self-confidence |
| Sympathy | Self-reliance |
| Patience | Self-respect |
| Force | Thrift |
| Determination | Resourcefulness |
| Firmness | Tact |
| Will Power | Judgment |

The above attributes represent only a small portion of the complete list—when we consider as well the combinations into which such attributes can be grouped into personalities—their number is beyond calculation.

It is evident, therefore, that this thing called personality is a subject which could never be dealt with in one single chapter—however long. So, I will not attempt to delve into psychology in a big way but rather confine this chapter to personality as it applies to selling.

Some say you shouldn't try to change an individual's personality. Some even say it's impossible because an adult is well beyond his formative years—and they may be right. However, I don't advocate changing it—I just think that you can improve your present personality by making it more sales-oriented. There are rules that can be followed to accomplish this. But first you must be aware of the fact that there are four kinds of personalities needed in selling:

1.  *The Engaging Personality*—Makes people like you.
2.  *The Assuring Personality*—Causes people to believe in you.
3.  *The Compelling Personality*—Gets people to act upon your recommendations.
4.  *The Dynamic Personality*—Makes you literally irresistible.

### Fitting your personality to your business

Different businesses require different personalities for the realization of maximum results. A business whose resistance is centered in the approach requires a personality which wins people—an engaging personality. If the resistance is centered in the demonstration, as is the case with a highly technical proposition or one which runs into considerable money, a personality which causes people to believe in you—an assuring personality—will enable you to get the greatest results.

If the resistance is centered in the close, you need a personality which induces people to act—a compelling personality.

If all elements are difficult, then you need a dynamic personality. It goes without saying, however, that if you really do have a dynamic personality, you will find selling in any business a relatively easy task. But very few are really dynamic.

### The engaging personality

An engaging personality, one which causes people to like you, is very helpful in all kinds of selling but it is indispensable in *competitive* selling where the demand is existent, all things are equal and the only question is which competitor will get the business.

If people like you, they go out of their way to do business with you. Here are two examples—one of which will hit home. We all frequent gasoline service stations—and what happens? As you drive up to the pump you run over the thin rubber hose which rings the bell inside the station. The attendant, with his feet up on the desk, is reading the sports page. He looks up with an annoyed expression, slowly brings his feet to the floor and ambles over to your side of the car.

"Please fill her up with high test," you say politely.

No answer.

He shoves the nozzle noisily into your tank and sets it at "slow." Then he leans on your car with his arms folded. If you're in a hurry, that's too bad. If you're lucky, he might clean your windshield. Ask him to check the oil and he makes another face. Finally the nozzle snaps. Your tank is full. But then he plays with it, on and off, on and off, to get another nickel's worth in. (The boss insists on this.) You pay him or charge it, you don't even get a "thank you" and you drive off in disgust. "And they call these *service* stations," you say to yourself.

Once in a great while you find a service station where the attendant jumps to his feet upon hearing the bell. He jogs up to you, greets you with a friendly smile, services your car, quickly and completely—and you are delighted. When he gives back your credit card, having noticed your name, he says, "Thank you very much, Mr. Jones, please come in again."

You like him for this. He handled you in a way that made you happy. And because he obviously had your interests at heart he made an excellent impression on you. Even if the gas he sells is one or two cents a gallon more than the competition, you will be glad to return whenever you possibly can. As we said, if people like you, they go out of their way to do business with you.

So, since the engaging personality is the type that makes people like you, here are the rules to follow in order to become more engaging:

### 1. Don't think or talk about yourself boastfully.

If your experiences and knowledge will be helpful to people, feel free to talk about them. But you must always use tact and avoid self praise. Don't talk about yourself merely because you enjoy it. Remember the time you had your brother-in-law over for dinner and he did nothing but talk about how great he is—and you became nauseous? Prospects or customers don't want to hear how great *you* are. In fact, they'd rather not talk about *you* at all. About *them?* Definitely.

### 2. Look for the good in everyone you meet and comment on it.

Get out of the habit of criticizing people—behind their backs. Instead—look for the good in a person and comment on it—to him—right on the spot. Amazingly enough you can always find something about a person you can like. (The worst crumb that ever walked the face of this earth —if you look hard enough—you'll find something about him you can like.)

If you follow this rule religiously—two things will happen. First of all you will endear yourself to everyone with whom you come in contact. Secondly, every time you find something good in somebody and you comment on it, a certain amount of that trait will automatically seep into your own personality. Do this—with everyone you meet and—if nothing else comes out of it—you will have at least improved upon your own personality.

*3. Look for a way to render a service.*

Trade something for the business you want. Suggest to the prospect a better way to do something he is now doing, or offer him an entirely new idea. If you can't do anything more, give him a spiritual lift. Make him feel better because you called. Say something that will brighten his day.

*4. Respect yourself, but don't fall in love with yourself.*

If you're good, admit it, even to yourself—for this builds up your respect and your confidence. But don't place yourself on a pedestal.

*5. Do not volunteer opinions.*

When you are selling keep your opinions to yourself on everything except your product or service. And be discreet in how you advance even those. If your opinions conflict with those of your prospect or customer—you automatically lose favor. What's the point? We all know that we should steer clear of sensitive subjects like politics and religion but there are countless other subjects which can easily turn into issues. Why get involved? It can prove very costly to you—even if you've won a point or two.

*6. Be considerate of everybody.*

Greet everyone you meet with a pleasant "hello" or a "hi." You never know who can help you to make a sale.

Also, develop the habit of saying "thank you" to everybody. We don't do enough of this. "Thank you" is something you can't say too often to people. They like being thanked even if it's repetitious. They feel that they're being appreciated and that's a very important feeling. Treat everybody with consideration and respect. Keep in mind that they are all human beings—regardless of their position in life. How do you speak to the garbage man— the same way you speak to your boss?

### 7. Smile.

Nothing spreads as much happiness as a pleasant smile. Not a silly grin that makes you look foolish. But a genuine smile that comes from really liking people. And you *should* like people. If you don't *really* like people—you've a problem. Chances are you don't belong in selling.

The people you call on have enough problems of their own to sadden their lives. Greeting them with a long face doesn't help them any. It certainly does nothing towards putting them in a buying mood.

### The assuring personality

The assuring personality causes people to *believe* in you and to accept your recommendations with confidence.

An assuring personality is a great asset in any kind of sales work but it is absolutely essential in creative selling, in which a desire for the product or service has to be created or crystallized. It is of great help to any salesman to develop a high degree of assurance in his personality; the result produced in the form of greater selling power will repay you a hundred times over for the effort required to develop it.

There are two rules to follow in developing an assuring personality:

*1. Master your product or service.*

Know your proposition thoroughly. Know what it will do; have evidence ready to prove your claims, you may need it; letters from users, incidents similar to the problem faced by your prospect, etc. Know all the competitive conditions in your industry. Study your proposition until you are an authority on it and the results it produces. There is no substitute for a complete and thorough knowledge of product or service in sales work.

I know that many salesmen don't want to become "a walking encyclopedia," and they find it easy to rationalize. Especially when the sales manager has said—"Look, it's impossible for you to know everything about our entire line." When you can't answer a question, level with the man and say, "I really don't know but I'll find out for you and get back to you tomorrow." Fine. It's good to level with people instead of trying to fake it. But how many times in an interview can you say "I don't know" and still expect the prospect to have faith in you? After three or four "I don't knows" he'd be justified in saying—"Listen, why don't you go back and first find out what your proposition is all about and then you can come back and try and sell it to me."

You just can't afford not to know as much as possible about whatever it is that you sell. Would you continue going to your doctor if you thought he didn't know enough about medicine?

*2. Never tell a lie.*

Almost sounds like kindergarten, doesn't it? Imagine suggesting to adults not to tell lies? And yet, in selling, the truth is not always easy to come by. It has been said that salesmen do to the truth what whipping does to cream. They change its consistency a little bit.

Don't do it. It isn't worth it. A little white lie here and there might get you an order. But in the long run you lose. You see, you can tell the truth for ten years straight to a customer—and he never comments on it because he expects it. But let him catch you in one single lie—and from then on he considers you a liar. He will never know whether or not to accept what you say. The standards are all gone. No matter what circumstances you find yourself in, always tell the truth. Everyone will respect you for your sincerity and truthfulness—and you'll have more respect for yourself. You will always be able to look people in the eye since you'll know that you have told no lies. Freedom from worry that a lie may come back to haunt you is important in selling. This peace of mind allows you to do a better selling job.

### The compelling personality

This is the one that enables you to get people to act upon your recommendations. It is a great asset. In fact it is practically indispensable in closing any and all kinds of sales. The greater the degree to which you develop it, the more successful you are bound to be in closing sales. Begin by learning these three simple rules:

#### 1. Develop a powerful self control

Expect and get things from yourself. You can only paint pictures of something you have seen. It is difficult to paint a picture of something you have never seen. If you want to expect and get things from others, you must begin by expecting as much from yourself.

Compel yourself to do the things you know you should regardless of how unpleasant they may be. If you have any bad habits holding you back, drive yourself into giving them up. If you have any bad selling habits, correct them at once. Either job is hard but the reward is great—well worth all the effort required.

If you want people to accept and act upon your recommendations, you must first drive yourself over the road you want them to travel. If you want to control others, you must first control yourself.

One of the most valuable habits a salesman can cultivate is that of thrift, the ability to have a little something even if it is no more than one dollar a week. It is not the amount that is important, it is the habit. It builds a little reserve which enables a man to be himself. Without a reserve he must be what he thinks someone else wants him to be. His opinions and his every action are influenced by his inability to take chances on any possible interruption to his income.

The habit of thrift is one of the most helpful habits a salesman can develop and still only a very small percentage have it. Why? Chiefly because it calls for sacrifice and to sacrifice one's self calls for self control, which is hard to develop. Thrift is a grand way to start the development of a complete self control. It will pay tremendous returns.

*2. Develop a determination that will not be denied*

Build up within yourself a quiet, inoffensive but inflexible determination which compels you to do every job you undertake as thoroughly, as completely and as accurately as it is possible for anyone to do it. A half-baked job reflects a half-baked determination; if you are half-baked in one thing, you will be half-baked in all things, including the handling of your sales. If you wish to inspire determina-

tion and action in others, you must first develop it in yourself; compel yourself to do every job as thoroughly, as completely and as accurately as anybody could possibly do that
particular job.

And keep your courage up. No matter how gloomy the
outlook may be, train yourself to keep trying. If the situation appears hopeless—at least give it a whirl. You will
be surprised at how often the *impossible* becomes possible.
Determination is built up within yourself through constant training.

A self-made, successful man was taking his son intown
to his office one day during school vacation. They were
walking the 8 blocks from their house to the bus stop and
noticed from a distance that the bus was coming speedily.
They started to run. Then Johnny said, "Dad, why are we
running, we're going to miss the bus." "I know," said his
father, "but let's miss it *trying*."

*3. Develop resourcefulness*

This enables you to think quickly and accurately on the
spot in critical situations. It comes mainly from reliving
your interviews. As soon as you've left the scene of a sales
call, review what was said for a few moments. Relive particularly the interviews in which you won—for those are
the ones you want to repeat. Don't spend very much time
thinking about the interviews in which you lost. If you
think about the positive, you will develop a positive personality and you will think about ways through which to
make more sales. This process will help you develop an
attitude of expectancy and great resourcefulness.

After you have imagined your way through a reasonable
number of interviews, you will find them starting to repeat
themselves and before you know it you will be ready for
almost any kind of sales situation which presents itself.

Your highly developed resourcefulness will be a pleasant surprise, as well as a source of many additional sales.

### The dynamic personality

There are, unfortunately, many salesmen who *think* they are dynamic (they really believe this because of an inflated ego). Actually the number of people in the entire world who are *really* dynamic is infinitesimal. Simply because to *be* dynamic one has to possess—or develop—a personality consisting of a balanced combination of all three of the types of personalities already discussed—the engaging, the assuring and the compelling.

Now, I said a *balanced* combination—and that's extremely important. If you work altogether too hard at getting people to like you, you could become sickening. If you overwork the assuring aspect—if you repeatedly tell the prospect "and I'm telling you the truth, and this *is* the truth"—he'll figure you must be lying. And if you become too compelling, you will come across too strongly, appear too pushy, and will most likely get thrown out.

So, to be dynamic you must have a *balanced* combination of the engaging, the assuring, and the compelling personalities—backed up by *confidence* and *enthusiasm*. Confidence comes from being certain that you will be able to accomplish something in the very way in which you planned it. Such confidence then develops into enthusiasm because you always like to do the things you do well.

You can develop a great deal of confidence and enthusiasm by projecting (and practicing), your interviews before you have them. A presentation pattern, well-designed, will enable you to plan the course of your interviews before you have them. When you realize that your interviews are coming out exactly as you had planned them, you will develop great confidence. The more this happens, the sooner you'll begin to radiate irresistible enthusiasm.

Without an abundance of confidence (aside from the personality aspect), selling can become a constant nightmare. Every time an interview is muffed and the prospect takes over, he wounds your pride. He tells you how he's been getting along without you very well for years and that you gave him no reason to change his mind. Or he boastfully tells you how he can buy the same product from one of your competitors at a much better price, with a better brand name to boot. When this happens a few times you begin to wonder if you can actually sell your product to anyone. Once this doubt creeps in, it becomes extremely difficult to maintain any amount of confidence, let alone develop more. The important thing to always remember is that confidence is something you can't buy. Neither can anyone give it to you or instill it in you. It is something that you must develop *on your own*. How do you do this? By having talks with yourself—privately, of course. Tell yourself that you *can* succeed. Tell yourself that if Joe Smith did this—so can you. Remind yourself that others with less on the ball than yourself have made it. Take stock of your attributes. Look in the mirror—if you present a good appearance, and you should at all times, compliment yourself. Tell yourself that you're just as good as the other fellow—maybe even better. Start being an optimist about yourself and about what you can accomplish. Remind yourself of your successes. Go over them in your mind in detail. Then tell yourself that you *can* do it again.

I repeat—confidence is something you must develop within yourself—there's no other way in which to get it. And it must be a continuing process in order to insure that you don't lose it.

While confidence is responsible for a substantial amount

of enthusiasm—almost automatically—it is still important that we discuss the role of enthusiasm in selling. Successful salesmanship and enthusiasm go hand in hand. Talk to a very successful salesman and note how electrifying his enthusiasm is—without a moment's let up. Being highly enthusiastic has two significant effects:

*a)*   It keeps the salesman "charged up."

*b)*   It stimulates the prospect and helps to convince him.

I learned this lesson very early in my selling career. My first job was with a small pharmaceutical manufacturer (Endo Laboratories, now owned by DuPont). It was so small in those days that the president of the company came to Boston to run the sales meetings himself. I'll never forget Joe Ushkow. He was unquestionably dynamic. A little guy whose presence always charged up the room— no matter how many people were in it. No one thought of him as a president. He was highly respected as a great salesman, and a leader of salesmen.

The first meeting I ever attended was held at the Hotel Statler in Boston on a Saturday morning. (They were always on a Saturday to avoid sacrificing week-day selling time.) There were fifteen salesmen present from all over New England and upstate New York. After Joe had quickly but politely greeted everybody with a handshake, a pleasant smile and a few warm words—he called the meeting to order. He said, "OK, men, let's start off by getting everybody to do a little thinking. I'm going to go up and down the rows (you'd think there were a hundred of them) and as I call on you—give me your definition of salesmanship."

Well, when you get hit between the eyes with a question like that first thing on a Saturday morning, it's not easy to quickly come up with a good answer. We scrambled. As each man came up with a poorly phrased, home-made definition—Joe would say, "Fine, that's part of it" and go on to the next salesman. He went through the whole group in about three minutes. Then he took a deep breath and —with a strong, projecting voice—he said, "Men, you're all on the right track, but let me give you my own personal definition. Salesmanship is nothing more than a 'transfer of enthusiasm.' If you can transfer *your* enthusiasm into the prospect, more often than not you've got a sale. That's been my experience over the years."

Every monthly sales meeting after that one was always opened dramatically. Joe Ushkow would call the meeting to order and then, at the top of his voice and waving his arms, he'd say, "OK, men, what's salesmanship?" The answer shook the walls of the room. It was loud, clear and enthusiastic. We would all shout back in unison: *"A transfer of enthusiasm."*

I'm sure you'll find many longer and more complete definitions for salesmanship. But how do you argue with success? We were working for a small, relatively unknown company. Our pharmaceutical products had trade names that doctors found hard to remember, simply because the advertising was sparse. We were bucking the giants like Lilly, Squibb, Parke Davis, etc. Yet we made inroads daily. Armed with all that enthusiasm that Joe instilled in us— we'd walk into a doctor's office and transmit most of it in a matter of minutes. We did the same with the druggists— in getting them to stock our products. With each commission check, our enthusiasm became even more magnetic. Each successive sales meeting had a similar effect. Our sales grew steadily and dramatically. So did the company.

Latch on to that word—*Enthusiasm*. Think about it constantly. Make sure your personality is loaded with enthusiasm. The rewards are great. So great that you will feel as though you're living in a different world. And you will be.

## Overcoming fear and its twin, the inferiority complex

Any discussion concerning sales personalities must give some consideration to fear and its twin bugaboo, the inferiority complex.

All salesmen, at some time, are troubled with fear in one form or another. Paradoxical as this may seem, it is something to be grateful for, as no man could be an outstanding salesman without encountering and overcoming this fear.

Fear is developed by the imagination. It is based on prejudgment and pride. You assume you are going to run into trouble and you imagine that you may be humiliated. Naturally you don't like it—no one does.

But you must make the call, you must have a sale, so you imagine what's going to happen. You rehearse the battle and when you are keyed up you go in, bristling, ready for the fray, with a chip on your shoulder. Your very attitude invites a challenge from your prospect.

There are two ways to overcome it. The first is to wear it down, to make calls often enough to learn that prospects are not waiting for you with a baseball bat in hand. The other way, the easy way, is to figure it out and realize that the first impression your prospect has of you or your proposition is the one you give him.

Realize that you are not going in to ask a favor, you are going to give as much as you get. You have nothing to hide, yours is an honorable proposition sold in an honorable way. Make the mental reservation that you are not going in to make a sale, you are going in to find out if the prospect needs what you're selling. If he has the need, you will tell him as much about it as he wants to know. If he does not need it, you will not try to sell it to him.

When you approach your prospects in that frame of mind, you realize that you are not involved in taking something away from them, but rather that you are rendering them a service. So, since there is nothing objectionable about what you are doing, there is absolutely nothing to fear.

Fear and an inferiority complex are founded entirely on self-created, false impressions. If you change the viewpoint, get control of the imagination, and direct it at the prospect's problems instead of thinking about yourself, fear and the inferiority complex will vanish into thin air almost immediately under the purifying influence of correct thinking.

There is one more aspect of personality directly related to fear and tension which must be discussed. Obviously, one of the best ways of displaying your personality is through your voice. Let's face it—your voice *is a part of your personality*. For this reason, therefore, your voice must be pleasing to the ear if you are to produce a good effect on the prospect. Research has shown that the lower the voice, the more pleasing it is to the ear. Conversely, the higher the voice, the more irritating it is to the person who is listening. Ever notice what happens to your voice when you are under stress or nervous tension? When you're trying very hard to make the sale? When you know you're not getting through to people and you're getting worried? The vocal chords seem to tighten up, your voice becomes higher, your enunciation is not as good as it was when you started, etc., etc., etc. How can you correct this? It's not hard. But it's a case of understanding exactly what's happening and how it can be corrected.

One of the chief reasons why we get tense is because we have a voluntary and an involuntary nervous system. You can control the voluntary system at will. Many of your muscles are in that system. For instance, you can move your fingers, your hands, other similar parts of your body, at will. Your involuntary nervous system, however, cannot be controlled at will. Your senses are in that system. If a sound occurs anywhere near you, you cannot avoid hearing it. If somebody walks near you with a bouquet of carnations, you cannot avoid smelling them.

Normally, the voluntary and the involuntary systems are in balance. Neither dominates the other. Under emotional stress, however, the involuntary system will dominate and this can cause many problems.

While you're reading this chapter, you are most likely very relaxed. You're very interested in the subject matter, you are enjoying the quiet around you, and you're thoroughly relaxed. But suppose I suddenly appeared before you and asked you to come with me. Suppose I took you for a ride across town to a theatre and suppose, after we walked in, I led you to the stage, introduced you to an audience of 1,000 people, and told them that you were there to deliver a 15-minute extemporaneous speech. What would happen to you?

As a normal individual your hands would perspire, you'd have a carload of butterflies in your stomach, your knees would tremble, and you would have serious trouble speaking, let alone thinking about what you want to say. And why does all this happen? It's caused by tension. Nervous tension. And, because you can't control your involuntary nervous system at will, there's very little you can do about it. That is, at that moment and under those circumstances.

Surprisingly enough, though, you *can* relax your involuntary nervous system. If you relax any muscle in your body, you also relax the nerve connected to that muscle and the nerve, in turn, relaxes the cells of the brain connected with the nerve. The diaphragm is the largest muscle in your body and is controlled by the involuntary nervous system. By relaxing the diaphragm you can exercise a relaxing influence throughout the involuntary nervous system. However, due to the fact that it is controlled by the involuntary nervous system, you cannot relax your diaphragm at will. But, since the diaphragm is the floor of your lungs, through specific breath control you *can* relax your diaphragm.

Technically, this is known as *diaphragmatic breathing*. It is the method of breathing and breath control which is mastered by all top-flight radio, television, and movie stars; opera and concert singers; public lecturers; and other such persons. They are constantly before large audiences. They can't afford to be under nervous stress nor can they afford to have the voice hampered in any way. So they depend on diaphragmatic breathing.

You must not deduce, at this point, that we're trying to change your method of breathing. Not at all. But if you learn to take only a dozen or so diaphragmatic breaths per day, your reward will be fantastic. Your voice will sound deeper and more resonant. And, as a bonus, you'll feel better.

How do you master diaphragmatic breathing? It's very easy, but let's understand the basic principles first. Place your left hand on your chest and your right hand on your stomach and take a deep breath. Observe that your chest comes out and the stomach pulls in when you inhale. Do it again. Isn't that exactly what happens? Remember, back in your school days, when the gym teacher would bellow: "O.K., now for some deep breathing exercises. Inhale—

stomach in, chest out." It was always, "Stomach in, chest out." O.K.! Take a deep breath by doing just that—and *hold it.* Note the feeling of tenseness in your back? That's muscular tension, which in turn creates nervous tension. Now exhale. As the chest goes down and the stomach fills out, the swelling of your stomach puts the tension on the diaphragm. That muscle rises to a dome in the middle and, because some of the abdominal organs are attached to it, when your stomach comes out it pulls down on this dome. When the dome is up, the diaphragm is relaxed. But when the dome is down, the diaphragm is tensed. Thus, during the 16 hours or more of each day that you are awake, you place a tension on the back when you inhale and on the diaphragm when you exhale. When you are sleeping you are in a much more relaxed condition; you are usually breathing more deeply and the diaphragm is not under tension.

By mastering the art of diaphragmatic breathing and by taking some diaphragmatic breaths while you are awake each day, you will be able to introduce an additional eight hours of relaxation into every day of your life. Whether you get that relaxation in a straight stretch of eight hours or whether you get it a few seconds at a time makes little difference. The beneficial effects are as great one way or the other. Thus, by the simple process of diaphragmatic breathing, you will be able to greatly increase your selling effectiveness not only because of your voice improvement, as you will learn later on, but also because you will be completely relaxed and, therefore, much more effective.

Now, once more, place your left hand on your chest and your right hand on your stomach and inhale. As we said, the chest comes up and the stomach pulls in. Exhale, and the chest goes down and the stomach comes out. Well, diaphragmatic breathing simply requires a slight change in that process. Place your left hand on your chest and your right hand on your stomach—but this time when you inhale don't pull your stomach in. Leave your chest alone and, as the air rushes into your lungs, push the stomach out. Observe how much more comfortable you feel. There is no muscular tension on your back. This is *diaphragmatic breathing*. See how simple it is?

To check yourself and make sure that you have caught on to diaphragmatic breathing, here's a simple test. Place both hands on your waist with fingertips touching. When you take a diaphragmatic breath—which means that you let your chest stay where it is but push your stomach out as you inhale—you will be able to separate the tips of your fingers as the air rushes in. When you exhale, the tips of your fingers will touch again. Repeat this a few times. It's a great way to prove to yourself that you now know how to breathe diaphragmatically. Removing all this tension from your entire body will greatly improve your voice. In fact, it will make you feel better, because diaphragmatic breathing increases the amount of oxygen in your blood stream. You probably will be surprised to learn that the bottom 20 percent of our lungs never do experience the luxury of real clean oxygen. Autopsies prove this. We just don't breathe deeply enough. Not enough to bring oxygen all the way to the bottom of our lungs. Through diaphragmatic breathing, you will bring much more oxygen into the lungs and that's the place where the oxygen is transferred to the capillaries of the bloodstream. The blood, in turn, carries the oxygen throughout the entire body. Results? A feeling of renewed vigor. Much more pep and energy. You won't get tired at 4 o'clock each day as you have in the past. You won't start yawning before the day is over.

Many times, when people are learning about diaphragmatic breathing and begin to practice the technique, they get dizzy. If this has happened to you, don't worry about it. It's simply because you are changing the mixture of oxygen and carbon dioxide in your lungs. You are increasing the oxygen and lowering the carbon dioxide. If you stop until the dizziness leaves you and then resume, you will soon be able to repeat the process of breathing diaphragmatically without causing any dizziness whatsoever.

As you can see, diaphragmatic breathing is not difficult to learn nor hard to master. It's simply a case of understanding it and then of making sure that you remember to take a number of diaphragmatic breaths each day. Get into a specific habit of taking diaphragmatic breaths at a special time each day. Some people take six or eight diaphragmatic breaths upon arising in the morning, then repeat this after lunch and once more after dinner. This is a good regimen and will help you greatly. But if you can get into the habit of taking the diaphragmatic breaths during the entire day at certain intervals, you will get even more benefit from it.

Here are a few ways in which you can remind yourself to do this. All of us open doors in the course of each day. Every time you reach for a doorknob make this a signal to take a diaphragmatic breath. If you do any amount of work on the telephone, every time you pick up a receiver to either answer or to call someone, take a diaphragmatic breath first. If you spend a considerable amount of each day in your automobile, you are apt to be stopped at a traffic light a number of times. Every time you're stopped, make the red light your signal to take a diaphragmatic breath. And don't worry about people who might be with you. Don't become self-conscious about this. Others will never notice what you're doing. They won't even notice that you're breathing differently than you usually do. It is a rare occasion when someone does notice and, if he does, he will assume that you're either sighing or taking a regular deep breath. He'll dismiss the whole thing without even discussing it with you. Remember? *Ninety-four percent* of the time, people are thinking about themselves.

When you get to the point that you can breathe diaphragmatically while you are speaking (and this doesn't take too much practice) and mouth your words as you are exhaling through your mouth, you'll amaze yourself. Your new, deeper, and richer voice, backed with more power, will project a new and better image. You'll have more confidence than ever, having reduced tension throughout your body. You will have found one more way through which to improve upon your personality.

You *can* develop a winning sales personality and, as you can see, it's done through deep thought and constant effort. It isn't easy. Nothing worthwhile ever is.

# CREATIVE SELLING

*There* are, as we said in Chapter 1, three types of sales; the *service sale*, the *negotiation sale* and the *creative sale*. The latter, of course, is the one that is brought about by the salesman who is able to sell something to someone who didn't realize he needed it. Many times he is able to come on the scene unexpectedly and in short order develop a need in the mind of the prospect.

### Creativity comes in many ways

If you look into the definition of "create" you find that it means "to cause to come into existence, to produce out

of nothing—to originate." I like the second one. To produce *out of nothing* is exactly what a salesman is doing
when he calls on someone unexpectedly and *creates* a
sale.

Now, this is not easy. It is difficult and it requires a
great deal of thinking—deep thinking—on the part of the
salesman. If it were easy, everybody would be using creative salesmanship and everybody would be extremely successful in selling. We know that this is not so. Creativity in
selling may take many forms, but in every case it is the
product of a good selling imagination. Your company cannot always supply the kind of selling imagination necessary to make a salesman highly creative. It is up to the
individual himself, when he is face to face with his prospect, to exercise the creativity that will put him and his
product over. I am reminded of a classic example of
creativity in selling designed entirely by a salesman to
whom it came very naturally. It happened some years ago
when one of our clients, Corning Glass, was introducing
shatter-proof glass. This was a very new kind of glass that
would not shatter into separate pieces but would simply
crack while remaining in one piece no matter how great
the force was that had been exerted on the glass. One of
their salesmen (in upstate New York) led the sales force
from the very first day the new glass was introduced.
Why? He was using creative salesmanship produced by
his own imagination. Instead of walking into the prospect's office and beginning a long harangue about the
great research that his company had done and how it had
been able to produce a glass that would not shatter, he
simply demonstrated very effectively and with a great
deal of showmanship what this shatter-proof glass was all
about.

Upon gaining admission in the prospect's office, he

would hold with his left hand a small piece of shatter-proof glass, whip out a hammer from his back pocket, then swing the hammer very emphatically and strike the glass. At that moment the prospect would jump for fear that pieces of glass would be flying towards his face. But, seconds later he would realize that the glass did not splatter and that this was a different kind of glass. More often than not this salesman got the order. He was just a little guy with a *big* creative mind.

We refined his presentation very slightly and then made sure that the entire sales force with Corning Glass was using this very same technique on every call. You would think that the rest of the salesmen would close the gap, sales-wise, between the creative whiz in upstate New York and themselves. But this didn't happen. That little guy was still forging ahead and leading by a greater margin than ever. When asked about it he said,

"Well, when I found out that the whole sales staff was going to be doing what I was doing I figured I had to do something a little bit better. So, now *I* hold the piece of glass but I give *the prospect* the hammer and I say, 'go ahead and whack it with all your might.' At first he hesitates. But there seems to be some psychological satisfaction that people derive when they themselves break glass. I have yet to have anyone refuse me. A few have said, 'we might get hurt.' But when I guarantee that they won't—they whack the glass with the hammer and are very pleasantly surprised. Then I write the order."

### The development of creative selling

As we have said, two elements come into play in the building of any sale. One is product knowledge, the other is you—the salesman. The product knowledge, in almost all cases, seems to be in great abundance mainly because companies do a good job in transmitting the facts about the product or service to be sold. As you read the bulletins, the manuals, the advertising matter, and attend the sales meetings, the conferences, and the conventions, these things continually implant more and more of the product knowledge in your mind. From your supervisor and fellow salesmen you may also learn the words and phrases which they are using with success about your product or service. You acquire their ideas on the presentation of certain benefits. If you take those ideas—and add a few different words of your own to further bring out the advantages your product or service has over competition —this *will* help to make you more successful, there is no question about that. But let's talk about the second thing. You, the salesman. To become a creative salesman you must follow a specific pattern. First of all, you must start doing your own thinking sales-wise. You must take ideas, analyze them, dig out the underlying principles, and determine the reactions they produce in the minds of prospects. This brings your sales imagination into full play. You can now take ideas from anybody in any type of selling and use them to sell your own product or service. Soon you develop the habit of analyzing everything from a sales standpoint. You study your procedures, your words and phrases, and smooth out your sentences. You add human interest and showmanship to your appeals. You study the aims, ambitions, and problems of each prospect or customer and learn how to match your appeals with their needs. You give them a clear picture of how they can use your product or service to achieve the results for which they are striving. You do all this while using strong words, convincing words, word-pictures, and imaginative phraseology. Your story—a creative story— becomes virtually irresistible.

Decide today that you will become a creative salesman and then work on it constantly—and think about it constantly. Soon you will get the idea. It will become easier and easier. Your mind will grow more creative as each day passes—as it does then you will begin to leave others behind, and your sales will zoom upward.

Many salesmen have asked me a significant question about creativity in salesmanship. *In what way can one train himself to think creatively?* There *is* a way—and it's an effective one. Just think of how many times in the course of one day you are exposed to advertising—the commercials on radio and television; billboards on the highways; the ads in your newspapers and all the magazines you skim through in waiting rooms; plus the mailings mixed in with your daily mail. Begin at once to pay more attention to all this advertising beamed at you. Analyze it. Try to determine what techniques are being used and why. What type audience is each one trying to reach? Why are certain phrases used? Are the colors significant? Were they pleasing to the eye or to the ear? Were they stimulating or intriguing?

You need not be interested in the product particularly —but *become* interested in the advertisement itself. What do *you* do when a commercial appears on your television set? Do you head for the lav or go to the refrigerator for another beer? If so, you are missing out on a great lesson on creative thinking—one that could very well help you get the sale the next morning.

**Three things determine your value as a salesman**

1. Technical knowledge
2. How much work you are willing to do (this along with 1 controls quantity of your salesmanship)
3. Personality (this element controls quality)

Let's consider how these three elements work together in producing a sale. Each time a pilot takes a plane aloft he must bring it back down safely. The first time he fails to make a safe landing he destroys the plane. A sales interview is very similar. Every time your prospect makes a statement of any kind your sale is up in the air and it must be brought down right side up. If you bring it down on its back just once during the entire sales interview you lose that sale. Each statement that your prospect makes goes into your ear and travels to your brain. There you formulate the answer which in turn comes out of your mouth. With that answer you either increase your chances of making that sale or you kill the sale. What you say in answer to any question depends entirely upon how well you are organized. Most of the time, when you are in an interview, you don't have the time to analyze the situation so thoroughly that you can come up with a perfect answer. Therefore, you must be ready with the right answers and your answers must carry the proper sales slant. It is quite possible for a salesman to answer a question one way and kill the sale and answer the same question in another way and make the sale—and in both instances he could be telling the exact truth. It is quite evident, therefore, that the development of a star salesman starts in the salesman's mind. So if you could take an x-ray of the brain of a successful salesman, it would show that he has a thoroughly organized knowledge of all the appeals and advantages of his product; that he is very familiar with all the shortcomings of his competition; that he keeps abreast of the conditions prevailing in the markets in which he sells; and that he has a good working knowledge of the problems, aims, and ambitions of his customers and prospects. As a result, during his interviews, he is able to take adavantage of every opening which will help him to get the sale. Furthermore, since he is able to figure out many advantageous ways in which his customers and prospects can use his product he *creates* countless sales. You would see in this x-ray of his brain that he knows the breakdown of the sale. That he realizes how there is an approach, a demonstration, and a close to every successful presentation. It would also be clear that, throughout the entire presentation, he knows exactly where he is and therefore he moves scientifically and steadily, step by step, towards the successful completion of the sale he is creating.

### Add organization to selling imagination

We have been talking about selling imagination. It is extremely important that you add *organization*. The big factor in organizing anything is to uncover the basic fundamental which makes it work. If you can crystallize clearly the fundamental that makes something work, the application of that fundamental becomes quite simple. Take flying, for example. Ever since man has walked the face of the earth, he has tried to fly. But after *6000* years we uncovered the basic fundamental that lets us fly. It consisted simply of creating a vacuum above and a lift below the wings of the plane while using a propeller or a jet engine to pull it through the air. With these three fundamentals, the plane can fly. In just a few decades we've certainly capitalized on these fundamentals. We can now fly faster than the speed of sound, we can lift over 350 tons in the air and we can fly in nearly any kind of weather.

What you understand about the basic fundamental of an approach, a demonstration, and a close, can be applied to any selling situation in which you find yourself. It will help you get the absolute maximum out of it. This kind of organization multiplies the value of everything to which it is applied. As an example, take iron ore. Suppose that it is worth $25 a ton. You organize it once, it comes out in the form of pig iron and it is now worth $50 a ton. Organize it again, into steel, and now it is worth $100 a ton. Organize it once again, now it's turned into razor blades and it is worth $10,000 a ton. Basically it is still iron ore. It has simply been organized several times and in the process its value has been multiplied several thousand-fold.

A new salesman is pretty much like iron ore. When he starts out he is thoroughly unorganized. He has very little product knowledge. But the company gives him all of the printed matter necessary to properly indoctrinate him. Usually they put him through a training course. Someone takes him out into the field so he can get an idea of the territory. His mind becomes filled with an abundance of facts—creating nothing but a big jumble. Early in a salesman's career he goes through a period of making call after call without realizing a single sale. But after a while he begins to organize this huge jumble of unrelated facts into meaningful information and he is then able to make some sort of a systematic presentation. Result? Once in a while he makes a sale.

If he makes 10 calls, he usually will get 3 interviews and he will make 1 sale. At this point he is a 10 percent salesman. If he keeps going and becomes more organized, things get brighter. (Particularly since every once in a while he musters enough courage to ask for an order.) Now he is a 15 percent salesman because if he makes the same 10 calls, he'll get the same 3 interviews but with a little more closing power; so he gets 1½ sales.

The next thing that happens is the most important—

he gets his approach organized. Now his story is interesting and more people will be willing to listen to him. He makes the same 10 calls, gets 9 interviews and makes 4½ sales. This makes him a 45 percent salesman. He is selling 4½ times as much as when he was working with information alone. Finally he gets quite skillful. He organizes everything. He cuts down the length of time he needs to go from one prospect to another. When he is face to face with the prospect he sells him in a fraction of the usual time. As a result, in the same length of time as it formerly took him to make 10 calls, he makes 20 calls with no more effort, gets the same ratio of interviews (18), the same ratio of closes (9) and now he is a 90 percent salesman (although he is still only selling 45 percent of his potential), because he has doubled the potential. Experience has shown that this is entirely possible.

### Sales are not accidents

Sales are not accidents—sales are built—first in your own mind and then in the mind of your prospect. Always remember that the mind of your prospect is the target for today, tomorrow, and the next day—and every selling day after that.

Every time you start out to make a sale you have begun a trip over a strange road. That road winds in and out of the subconscious mind of your prospect. Your destination is his Hot Button. Now, if you were starting out on a trip in your automobile, over a strange road, going to a destination where you had never been before, what would be the first thing you would do? Wouldn't you consult a road map? With it you could organize the trip on paper before you even started. Say you were going from New York to Caribou, Maine. You could begin with the knowledge that it is approximately 450 miles northeast of New York and you would eventually get there after making several detours and wasting a great deal of time and effort. But you would have arrived there much sooner if you had organized the trip with the aid of a road map knowing exactly which route to take from beginning to end. Similarly, if you go into your interviews unorganized, depending solely on your enthusiasm and your determination, you will get some sales, but you won't get anywhere near as many of them as when you are thoroughly organized— nor as quickly either.

There are certain reactions that must take place in the mind of the prospect if you are to sell him. They are your road markers throughout the trip which you take through his subconscious mind. First of all the prospect must decide to listen to you. And it is up to you as a salesman to get him to *listen* with his mind as well as his ears in order for him to *absorb* your idea. Then the prospect has to believe your statements so that he can *accept* them. After that he has to be able to see how your proposition *applies* to what he is trying to do. And finally, you have to influence his mind to the point that he is willing to *act* now. Remember these reactions which must take place in the mind of the prospect if you are going to bring the sale into existence, you must get him to listen, to absorb, to accept, to apply, and to act.

Perhaps you think that this is almost impossible to do. It is not. You can positively influence the prospect's thinking. You can lay a track on which the interview will run so that you can exercise full control. That track will consist of the answers to the five questions that go through the mind of every prospect. He never asks these questions. He never even asks them of himself because they are too deeply imbedded in his subconscious mind. But they are there and they must be answered or you won't be able to sell him. If you leave any one of these questions unanswered, you make it necessary for him to dig deeply for the answers on his own—and this he rarely will do.

### The five W's

What are these five questions? The first of them is the question "*Why?*" The first thing that goes through the subconscious mind of a prospect when you come on the scene is "Why should I listen to this salesman? Why should I give him the time to make his presentation?" The best answer for this is quite simple when you think about it. Give him a quick glimpse of the end result which you will produce for him if he lets you tell the rest of the story. Let me give you an example.

One of the men who had taken our sales course in Boston worked for the Boston Envelope Company and he sold drinking cups. His name was Ray Vinson. He had an opportunity to bid on one million drinking cups which were to be sold to the American Optical Company for distribution to their branches throughout the country. Ray bid $1600.

He was one of five men who were to have 10 minutes before the purchasing committee to explain the merits of the bids submitted. But before he went into the meeting, one of his friends who worked in the purchasing department said to him, "Ray, you haven't got a chance. They have already decided against you. Your bid for $1600 is $600 higher than the next bid. And the others are all under that. They have already ruled you out." That didn't bother Ray because he had the answer to the question *"Why"* at his fingertips. He stepped into the meeting and said to the purchasing committee,

"Gentlemen, my drinking cup has a big advantage over all the others. The edge is crimped and it can't cut the lip of the drinker. If you buy any other drinking cup, sooner or later your workmen will cut their lips on the sharp edges of the cups. As they brush the blood away with the back of the hand, dust and glass flying about in the manufacture of spectacles and lenses will be deposited in the cut and an infection will be started. An employee may be out for two weeks or more, *at your expense.*"

The Vice President and Chairman of the purchasing committee remembered an incident very similar to the one Ray described. He said, "Son, you've got something" and Vinson walked out of that meeting with an order for $3200 worth of drinking cups.

If you are not opening your interviews in this way now, I would recommend that you begin doing so at once regardless of what you are trying to sell. Remember, always give the prospect a quick glimpse of the end result.

The next question which must be answered for the prospect is—*"What is it?"* Many salesmen like to keep him in suspense. They take far too much time leading up to what the product or service actually is. Often this proves to be antagonizing. You should waste no time in stating what it is that you wish to sell him. As soon as you have given him a quick glimpse of the end result (in answering the question *"Why"*), explain in crisp, simple terms how this end result can be obtained by using your product. Remember, he's busy and he appreciates your getting to the point as quickly as possible.

At this point the prospect wants to know *"Who says*

*so?"* It is important for him to know who is responsible
for the claims and promises that you are making. Here is
where the name of your company comes in. It isn't that
you try to disguise whom you work for—that's something
to be very proud of. But you must realize that the name of
your company does not do the selling. It only gives the
prospect the confidence to do business with you after
something else has sold him on the idea. That something
else is the answer to the questions, *"Why"* and *"What is
it."* After that, the name of the company, and your name
as well, become of interest to him. But when you do
bring in the name of your company, do it as creatively as
you can. For instance, let's say your company has been in
business for 90 years. Don't just say, "We've been in
business 90 years." That's colorless. Say something like—
"For almost a *solid century* we've been a growing, successful company." Now, you see, when a company like *that*
makes a claim, it's usually true. Also, if you show him
literature and reprints, making the very same claims you
stated, you've erased any doubt in his mind.

The next question is *"Who did it?"* He wants to know
who has used this product or service and had satisfactory
results with it. He doesn't want to be a pioneer. This part
of selling is actually a gold mine that many salesmen overlook. It has tremendous power. Nothing you can say, at
this point, will have the impact of testimonial letters
from companies respected by the prospect.

Finally, the prospect wants to know *"What do I get?"*
This is where you add it all up. This is actually the *close.*
Many think that the closing of a sale is a duel to the bit-
ter end between the prospect and the salesman during
which the salesman gets the prospect to finally sign on the
dotted line just before they both topple over in an exhausted heap. That's the hard way. The easy way is to

get to the prospect's Hot Button as early in the interview as possible and then just keep banging away at it.

Now, let's add up what we've said so that we won't ever forget the five W's. They are:

Why?
What is it?
Who says so?
Who did it?
What do I get?

And this is how it all works: You answer the question *Why?*, the prospect decides to *listen* and you've reached his ear. You answer the question *What is it?*, he is able to *absorb* and understand your idea and now you move into his subconscious mind. You answer the question *Who says so?*, he sees that there is responsibility behind your promises and he *accepts* your statements. You answer the question *Who did it?*, he is able to see how he can *apply* this to what he is trying to do and you pass another milestone. You answer the question *What do I get?*, and now the sale is complete. He decides to *act*. You are on his Hot Button. All that is needed now is the hook-up from the Hot Button in his mind to his mouth. He says, "OK" and out comes your sale.

This "5W" formula is what brings creative sales into existence. It has increased the salary and the income of tens of thousands of salesmen. Many businesses have installed this formula from top to bottom in every branch of the business and become the leaders in their industries. Anyone who has made the effort to organize a presentation around these 5W's has been repaid one thousand fold.

Give this presentation pattern the toughest test you possibly can. Organize a presentation on your product based on the 5W's for a desirable prospect whom you have been unable to sell. Present it to him as soon as possible. You will be delighted at how much you have added to your selling power. Then, if you use it in every single sales interview, you will send your sales and income zooming skyward almost immediately. You simply can't miss.

# THE APPROACH

*If you* have gray hair—or if you're just beginning to get a few at the temples—you will remember the days when automobiles did not come with automatic transmissions. The left foot was kept busy (with a clutch pedal) and there was a stick shift on the floor or under the steering wheel. Modern science hadn't yet invented the automatic transmission and driving was quite different (although nowadays the standard type is coming back—like 4 on the floor—because we need something to do while we're driving). With a standard shift it was necessary to go through a specific routine when starting from a stopped position. First you would shift into first speed, lift the clutch and give it some gas—to get the car in motion; then you would shift into second in order to gain

57

more momentum; and, finally (when you were reasonably certain that the car wouldn't buck like a bronco), you would shift into third and you were all set—until you came to a stop. Then you'd start all over again—first, second, third, in that order—and always in that order.

Selling is very much like that. There are three parts to *any* sale (and it doesn't matter whether you sell a product or a service). They are 1) the *approach,* 2) the *demonstration,* and 3) the *close.* In the approach you get the prospect's or customer's *interest.* In the demonstration you *convince* him that your product or service is best for him. In the close you *persuade* him to take action now. How does this compare to driving a car? The three parts of the sale must always come in that order. And every time you come face to face with a prospect (or even a regular customer) you must start all over again—with the approach.

Without question the approach is the most important part of any sale. Many will argue that the close is the most important part. They'll rationalize that in the close you get the order, and that's most important. Nonsense. With a successful approach you get the prospect's interest. Without his interest you never get to the close. And there won't *be* an order.

### Why you need an effective approach

The main objective of the approach is to get the prospect's interest by making him see that he needs some advantage which he does not enjoy now. Your success as a creative salesman depends to a great degree on your ability to make an effective approach to each prospect. Why? Because the approach determines how many times you will get a chance to make a presentation, how receptive the prospect will be, how welcome you will be on call-backs, and how difficult (or easy) the close will be for you. I might add that our experience has shown that when the approach is based on the correct principles, you will get in to see three times as many prospects as you are accustomed to seeing. And you will, therefore, make three times as many sales and progress three times as fast as you ordinarily would have. That's just plain arithmetic.

Not only is the approach the most important part of any sale—but the first 30 seconds of your approach are crucial, critical, pivotal. Because—in that very short span of time—a great deal happens. I'm sure you know about first impressions and how costly they can be. But aside from that, in the first 30 seconds of a sales interview the prospect makes a big decision. If what you've said is of interest to him, he decides to listen to the rest of your presentation. If, on the other hand, your approach did not gain his interest—he decides that he isn't going to listen to the rest of your presentation. You won't necessarily get thrown out—in fact—most people are polite. They never throw you out—they just *tolerate* you. And 20 minutes later you're still there reciting all of the benefits and features of your product. You may still be there *physically*—but, as far as the prospect is concerned, you might as well have gone home. He has simply tuned you out.

Let's get one thing straight regarding the approach right here and now—whenever you make an approach and the prospect comes back with, "I'm not interested," you are simply getting the correct answer to what you said. Because, if what you had said had been interesting to the prospect, then he couldn't possibly have said to you, "I'm not interested."

You must learn to start blaming yourself. It is very easy to quickly assume that the prospect is an idiot, that he has a closed mind, that he doesn't understand new ways of doing things, etc. These are all rationalizations. It is a lot harder to ask yourself, why you got the answer, "I'm not interested." Obviously, you didn't impress him and certainly didn't get his interest. So you say, "I must brush up on my approach." As soon as you begin to think this way and start talking to yourself in this fashion, you will begin to make approaches that are much more effective. They will have been planned in advance and they will be designed to catch the prospect's interest in the very first 30 seconds.

You will probably be surprised to learn that 95 percent of the salesmen in this country don't have an approach. They *think* they do, but they are presenting themselves and their product or service in such a weak fashion that it just simply doesn't represent an approach at all. They rush to get themselves face to face with the prospect and at that point they say, "My name is . . ., I'm from the ABC Company and I came here because . . ." By this time the prospect has figured out how to get rid of the salesman. Why is this approach so weak? The prospect is not interested in your name. If he never saw you before and never heard of you, your name is of absolutely no significance to him. There is no reason why he should make an effort to try and remember it. If the name of your company is also foreign to him, he will make no specific effort to try and find out more about it. Even if you represent a large, well-known company, he still is not terribly excited about it, particularly if he didn't send for you. And if he has problems on his mind, which is usually the case, he would have trouble repeating what you said in the first several sentences because he most likely wasn't listening at all.

I know exactly what you're thinking. You are probably

saying to yourself, "Well, what am I supposed to do, go in incognito?" Not at all. Of course you tell the prospect who you are and the company you represent, but it simply doesn't belong in the first sentence. The first thing you should do is to say something that will gain his interest from the standpoint of *what's in it for him.* After that, you tell him who you are and who you represent. He will be more interested in your name and the name of your company, particularly if he can already see that you can do something of value for him.

A well-planned approach sets out to accomplish the following things:

1. Neutralize the prospect's mind.
2. Plant the idea you want to sell.
3. Satisfy his reason (by winning his confidence and justifying the time needed to make the complete presentation).
4. Determine his chief ambition (his Hot Button).
5. Crystallize his need for your product or service.

The sequence is extremely important. The five steps should always come in this order and everything you say should be calculated to bring about the necessary effect.

You are probably wondering how you can possibly do all this in the first 30 seconds. Well, we didn't say that. We said that the first 30 seconds were the most important part of the approach. And in that short span of time you should attempt to do one thing, and one thing alone. You should neutralize his mind. What does this mean? It's very easy to make it clear. Whenever you call on a prospect or customer he invariably has many important things on his mind. Some of these things are good things (like the fun he had last night at the party he attended, or the great round of golf he had yesterday, or the new car he is buying), more often, however, he has problems on his mind. These cause him constant worry, constant concern. The business isn't doing so well, his boss is applying more pressure than ever, his assistant just resigned, and on top of all this, there might be personal problems, family problems. Perhaps your prospect had a big argument with his wife on the telephone just before you came in. When you take all this into consideration, I am sure you can see that your coming in and opening with, "My name is, I'm from the ABC Company and I came here because". . ., will give him absolutely no reason to stop thinking about the problems on his mind. And until he does he won't start thinking about the things *you* want to talk to him about. Therefore, in the first 30 seconds you must, in crisp, concise language, say something (other than your name) that will immediately intrigue his imagination and thereby neutralize his mind. Then you proceed with the rest of your approach and your presentation, knowing full well that he's listening all the way.

In case this whole idea is a little foreign to you, don't close your mind by deciding that it's impossible to approach people and start a conversation without first introducing yourself. Who said you *must* introduce yourself first? Who made such a strict rule which you feel you must follow? Forget it. Don't be so formal. Don't do something just because everyone else does, and it seems to be the thing to do. There is absolutely no reason in the world why you can't approach *anybody* with a pleasant smile, a firm handshake and a planned statement designed to neutralize his mind. When you ask a stranger for directions or information, do you introduce yourself first? Not necessary, is it? Remember that some of the most interesting conversations you have had were with strangers while waiting in line somewhere. And do you remember what happened just before parting? You ended up exchanging business cards or simply introducing each other. And why? Because you became interested in each other and now the names, home towns, and your lines of business became important. Throughout most of the conversation, however, it didn't matter, did it? These are modern times. Formality in professional selling is no longer required. Accept it as fact.

## Selecting the right approach

There are three types of approaches you can use which will neutralize the prospect's mind and start you off on a successful sale. The first of these, and perhaps the most effective, is based on *curiosity*. It takes advantage of a very significant human phenomenon. Everyone, and I mean *everyone,* is curious to an amazing degree. You can make this observation almost any time, anywhere. For instance. You're driving along a highway and a few miles down the road you can see smoke going up into the sky. When you get closer you find that there is practically a traffic jam. Why? Everyone wants to stop and look at the fire. No one is doing very much about it, but they want to look. In fact, there will be so many curious people at the scene that many times the fire fighters have trouble getting through. The same thing happens when there is an accident. While the traffic backup may be caused because one lane is tied up, what really slows things down is the fact that each curious motorist proceeds very, very slowly so that he can take a good, long look at what has happened. Some have even pulled to the side of the road and stopped. They simply don't want to miss anything that's going on. Many of these people claim that they are always in a hurry—but there always seems to be time to satisfy one's curiosity. So if you open an interview with an approach based on curiosity, your chances of neutralizing the prospect's mind are great. All you need to do is to develop an opening statement which makes the prospect want to know more about what you're selling. But it must relate to your product or service—otherwise, you will have tricked the prospect—and this he won't like.

Here is an example. An extremely successful salesman who uses a curiosity approach in selling insulation to home owners does it this way. He knocks on the door. The lady answers. He looks her in the eye and says, "Good morning, do you know what the laziest thing in the world is?" The woman is so surprised at this approach that she doesn't know what to say. But she's curious. So she says, "What *is* the laziest thing in the world?" And he replies, "It's a dollar bill hidden away in your cookie jar doing nothing when it could be earning you 20 percent." She says, "What do you mean?" And then he goes on to explain how by insulating her home she would save at least 20 percent on her heating bill which in turn would give her extra money for clothes, eating out and other wants.

Invariably, with this impactful approach, he is able to convince her that he should come back on a specified evening to sit down with her and her good husband and discuss the possible insulation of their home in greater detail. When he comes back the ground work has been done for him. The wife has already convinced her husband that they should sit down and discuss it because she keeps thinking of the 20 percent saving and how the extra money will stretch the household budget. More often than not he is able to make the sale. It's not easy to sell insulation house to house, you will agree, but with a curiosity approach and by hitting the Hot Button of the woman in the house when he mentions *extra clothes for her,* success is not hard to come by.

Another good way of using a curiosity approach is to call your product or service by another name,—a name that no one else has ever heard of before. Like the dictating machine salesman who opens with, "Did you ever see a mind eraser?" The prospect replies with the only thing he can say,—"What the heck is a mind eraser?"

"It's a little machine," says the salesman, "but it will do wonders for you. For instance, you get an idea and you don't want to lose it, or you decide to write a note to someone before you forget about it. You pick up my machine and you record it. Now you don't have to worry about forgetting it because it's there permanently for you or your secretary to do something about. It's a mind eraser, isn't it?"

Invariably the prospect is intrigued. He is stimulated by such an unusual approach. There is no question that his mind has been neutralized and the salesman is working on an open mind, a mind that can be sold. Surely you will agree that this is a far better approach than if the salesman had said, "Good morning, Mr. Jones, I'm from the ABC Company, we make dictating equipment and I'd like to tell you why ours is the best on the market." That type of approach brings about the answer, "I'm not interested" or "We don't need any."

That's why, in their advertising, large companies go out of their way to give their well-known products a new and different name. That's why IBM, as an example, calls its computer a "mind extender." Beachcraft calls an airplane a "multiplying machine." (When you read the copy you find that when buying a corporate plane you are able to multiply your executives immediately. They can be in more places in less time.) The John Deere Company calls its riding lawnmower a "weekend freedom machine." There is no end to what you can do in creatively renaming your product or service. It just takes a little thought on your part and you can equip yourself with the most impactful curiosity approach possible.

Here's another type of approach. It's based on *appreciation*. Everybody likes to be appreciated. It will be extremely rare when you meet someone who doesn't enjoy being appreciated. Now this doesn't mean that you flatter people—because flattery is insincere. It's a form of lying. We have already said that a professional salesman should never tell a lie. In using appreciation, you merely remark favorably and truthfully on something you like. For instance, you can appreciate a man's tie by commenting upon its color or design. You can appreciate a woman's hairdo or the color of her dress or the flower on her desk or a piece of jewelry she may be wearing.

Not too long ago I was working with a salesman out in the field. He told me how he had gone to a large company on several occasions but couldn't get to see a man no matter what he did. He had tremendous buying authority but this salesman just couldn't get to him. I asked how come? He said, "Because he has an old battle ax of a secretary who refuses to let me get into his office. Every time I go there I give her my card, she looks it over, decides that Mr. Jones wouldn't be interested and that's the end of the possible sales call." I suggested that we try it together. I explained that he should let me handle the secretary and once we got into Mr. Jones' office then he could take over with selling his proposition.

When we got there it was worse than I had anticipated. She was definitely a battle ax. Meanness was written all over her face and her penetrating look was frightening

As I came closer to her I noticed a most unusual wristwatch which she was wearing. It had rubies and emeralds and diamond chips. Clearly it was one of a kind. I said to her, without a greeting of any kind, "Isn't that a most unusual watch." A big smile came across her face. A smile that I never would have thought possible on someone like her. She said, "Do you like it?" I said, "I've never seen one like it. It's just simply beautiful." "It was my grandmother's," she replied, "and I treasure it."

Well, we talked about it for a minute or two as the atmosphere about us became warmer and friendlier. At the opportune moment, and almost in a whisper, I said, "We'd like to see Mr. Jones. Could you arrange it for us?" She said, "You just wait right here." She went into the inner office for a matter of seconds, came out and ushered us in. She never asked for our names, never questioned what we were there for, didn't even recognize my friend who had been there several times. And why? Because she was engrossed in a discussion over the watch which *she* owned, which *she* treasured and which *she* enjoyed having appreciated. It's amazing how people will react when handled properly through an approach based on appreciation.

If you call on retail stores and the owner has just remodeled his place of business, you have an excellent opportunity to appreciate the job he did. He will like you for it and it certainly will neutralize his mind. Besides, few people will have commented on his remodeling job and he wants to know how people feel about its outcome. He also knows how great an investment it represents and he's delighted when people notice it. The same is true when a company has built a new building or an executive has remodeled his office or bought new furniture There is only one catch in the using of approaches based on appreciation. Since people love to talk about themselves or something they own, you can end up spending too much of your time doing just that. You must make sure that soon after completing a successful approach based on appreciation you smoothly change the subject to just how the prospect can profit by using your product or service.

A third type of approach is based on *customer or prospect interest*. You give the person you approach a quick glimpse of the end result. You open with statements such as, "In just a few minutes I can show you how your overhead can be cut by at least 15 percent" or "we can increase your profit by 10 percent" or "by $50,000" or "your shipping expenses will be cut in half." There are very few people who won't want to listen to more of your story after an opening like that. But you can and should make it even more dramatic if you work at it. Suppose you are selling a piece of equipment to industry which will cut down their production costs. Let's assume that your equipment will bring about a savings, according to their production which you have estimated, of approximately $200 a week. That's $10,400 per year. You walk in, look the man right in the eye, and while shaking hands pleasantly say, "Good morning, Mr. Jones, I came here today to give you $10,400." The normal response will be, "How are you going to do that?" And you're off with your presentation.

It will give you a strange feeling to use an approach like this—this is only natural. In fact, developing approaches such as we have been discussing will give you many a strange feeling. It's so different from what you've been doing—routinely. But simply remember one thing —you would also have strange feelings if you dressed or acted as peculiarly as some of the comedians do on television. Yet, you would very soon get used to it. The size of your bank deposits would materially help you in making the adjustment.

Becoming proficient in all three types of approaches is a must for a professional salesman. Familiarize yourself with every possible usage of them and then continue to develop new and different approaches as time goes on. Some people find an approach which works successfully and then stick to it indefinitely. While this theory makes sense when calling on new prospects, it is not feasible with regular customers. Don't make the mistake that so many salesmen do regarding regular customers. Because they are calling on an individual on a weekly, monthly or any other regular basis, they assume that an approach is no longer necessary. This is a big mistake. The approach remains the most important part of any sale regardless of how many times you call on the same individual. Just because you get to know a regular customer is no reason to assume that the niceties of "How are you, how have you been," are ample as far as an approach is concerned. His mind must be neutralized each time you call on him. The best way to accomplish that is to always begin with a new and fresh approach. You can rest assured that he won't object to it—he might comment—but even that is rare. In fact, he will soon get used to the whole idea, and he'll be looking forward to your next visit if for no other reason than to note just what type of an approach you'll use on him this time. Sure, you'll feel funny doing this with a regular customer. It will be rather foreign to you at first, but soon it will become second nature. You will gain new stimulation for yourself in your work every time that you force yourself to come up with a new and different approach on an old customer.

### When all other approaches fail . . . shock 'em

Some of the biggest and best sales have been made by individuals who went off the deep end to get somebody's interest and attention. The following true story proves this point most conclusively.

Saul Lehman, a good friend of mine, came to the U.S. back in the early 20's at the age of 18. He brought along his mother and all of their personal belongings. Everything they owned was in a single suitcase. Without a father and without money, it immediately became his responsibility to furnish support for himself and his mother and to make something of himself career-wise. He decided to learn a trade and obtained a job in a printing company as an apprentice. His ultimate goal was to become a compositor. He soon realized that he would never be able to make much money working for someone else as a compositor so he saved every dollar that he possibly could.

After a few years, he struck out on his own. He bought himself a small printing press and began to operate a one-man business. He would go out and take orders for calling cards, stationery, envelopes or invitations, come back to his small shop, print the job and then deliver it and collect his money.

One day he learned that the Hearst newspaper organization bought a great deal of printing. He was amazed because he assumed that they did their own. But, a newspaper prints newspapers on its large presses and the small printing jobs were farmed out. He found out that the buyer would only see salesmen on Tuesdays from 1 to 3 P.M. The very next Tuesday Saul was there at 12:45 so he would be the first salesman to be interviewed. He gave his calling card to the buyer's secretary and at 1 o'clock sharp he was allowed to go into the inner office. The buyer had a long, narrow office with his desk at the very end. Saul walked briskly the length of the office, shook hands with the buyer and then proceeded to explain what he could do for him. He showed samples of his work, quoted his most reasonable prices, displayed a great deal of warmth and asked for the order. The answer was, "We're all set for the time being, we'll let you know when we need some printing done."

Every two weeks Saul went back and each time he received the very same answer. After the fourth visit Saul realized that each visit had been exactly the same as the first one. The buyer wouldn't recognize him, he would have to start from the very beginning and explain who he was, etc. and it was quite obvious that he had made no impression whatsoever. So, he made a big decision. He simply had to go all out to get this man's interest and attention.

He went to a pawn shop and bought a used derby hat for 29 cents. The next Tuesday, at 12:45, he was in the waiting room sitting erectly with his derby hat under his left arm. As usual, at 1 P.M. he was told to go in. He walked halfway down the long, narrow office, carefully placed the derby hat on the floor, raised his right leg up high and faced the buyer. He said, "My name is Saul Lehman." With a thumping noise he stepped on his derby hat, made an about face and proceeded to walk out of the office. The buyer screamed "Wait just one minute. What's the idea of coming into my office and stomping on your derby hat?" Turning, Saul smiled and explained:

"Four times I've come in to see you and each time it was as though I were a stranger. You never remembered me from the time before, you never remembered my name and you never rememberd anything that I said. I had to make an impression. This was the only thing I could come up with. It was a second-hand, 29-cent hat. At least now you'll remember me as the guy who stepped on his derby hat."

The buyer burst into laughter. He said, "Come over to my desk and sit down." They chatted for a few minutes and Saul got his first order. Every time he came in after that they would laugh about the derby hat episode and the orders kept getting larger.

There was so much talk at the newspaper about the man who steped on his hat that the story finally got to William Randolph Hearst himself. He was so intrigued that he asked to meet Saul Lehman when next he came in. The following Tuesday Saul arrived at 12:45. He was told by the secretary that Mr. Hearst wanted to see him. Saul almost panicked. He asked, "Did I do something wrong? Did I foul up a job?" "I don't think so," said the secretary, "he simply wants to meet you." Saul was relieved. He walked into the boss' office where Hearst gave him a very warm welcome.

Hearst had him sit down and tell the whole story concerning the derby hat after which they both laughed heartily. Hearst was an impulsive individual and took an immediate liking to Saul Lehman. He looked him in the eye and he said, "If I could give you the thing you want most right now, what would it be?" Saul smiled and coolly said, "Fifty thousand dollars." "What would you do with it?" was Hearst's snappy reply. Saul had the answer ready: "I would buy two big, beautiful presses and then would I ever be able to put out the printing." Hearst gave him a check for $50,000 and said, "Here you are. You can return it to me when you earn it back."

That was the turning point in Saul's life. He bought the presses and he was on his way. As the years went by Saul became one of the largest printers in the New York area. As owner of the Georgian Press on Varick Street, in the printing district, Saul kept an army of printers busy, 3 shifts around the clock, in a 10-story building fully equipped from top to bottom. A few years ago he invited me to a luncheon in honor of his son's birthday. He praised Jesse to the large gathering and announced that the birthday present was "the building across the street with the bank in it." Saul made himself a millionaire. He attributes every inch of his success to the day he stepped on his derby hat and made an impression with an unusual approach.

Here's another example from a different industry. The most successful life insurance company in Japan is owned by a man who claims that his success is due to his capitalizing on a rare sales aproach. This is how he does it.

He hires only women—and they must be widows. He sends them out selling life insurance door to door—at night—because the man of the house is most apt to be home then. When the husband opens the door,—the woman doesn't say, "My name is, I'm from the ABC Company and I came here because . . ." She simply looks him in the eye, says absolutely nothing—and then looks down and proceeds to open her purse. She takes out what looks like an insurance policy (it has Life Insurance written all over it), raises her eyes and says, "If my husband had bought this for me, I wouldn't have to be here tonight trying to sell it to you." The man shudders. He can practically see his wife as a widow going door to door on a rainy night, trying to sell insurance simply because he hadn't provided for her, and he lets her in.

By now you should be convinced that you must, at once, begin to concentrate on your approach. With a good approach, a handshake and a smile you will have vastly increased your effectiveness. And speaking of the handshake, let's clearly understand its importance. It transmits warmth and friendliness. It breaks down barriers. It's a good climate creator. Adopt a policy of shaking hands with everyone at the *beginning* of the interview and at the *end* of the interview. And I mean *everyone*. Women included. The books on etiquette state that you shouldn't shake hands with a lady until she first extends her own hand. Forget it. I have been shaking hands with women for years and I have yet to be turned down. They remember you for it. Why are we so formal with a lady in the U.S.? In other countries men will kiss her hand (or pinch her fanny), and she likes it. Here in the U.S. we stand far apart, click the heels, bow the head and say, "Pleased to meet you" or, "How do you do?" How cold. How stuffy. Start shaking hands with receptionists, secretaries, lady buyers, prospects' wives, etc. That kind of body contact will never get you into any trouble.

One more point. Avoid flashing your calling card every time you make an approach. As a matter of fact, don't use your calling card until you absolutely have to. It will never make a sale for you. I sometimes wonder if the calling card wasn't invented by printers to keep themselves in business. You know as well as anyone else that when a prospect says, "Let me have your card" or "Leave me your card and we'll call you," he is simply going through the motions. The minute you walk out it goes into the round file. When you do leave your calling card, make sure you do two things with it. First, write the prospect's name on it. ("For Mr. Jack Jones . . .") Then include a bit of helpful information such as a quote. It will be difficult for him to dispose of it too quickly because he hates to throw away anything bearing his name. Also, the information you wrote on the card might be of importance to him later on and this might prompt him to save the card—at least for a few days.

Maybe you think that leaving your calling card is worthwhile—because buyers save them. Well, a friend of mine designed a special box in which buyers could file salesmen's cards. The box was good looking and it had two sections—one for filing by company and the other for filing by the man's name. But he soon discovered an important fact. There was absolutely no market for them.

# THE DEMONSTRATION

*A*fter a successful approach you immediately slide into the second part of any sale, the demonstration. Now this is not necessarily a physical manifestation. The word, demonstration, is used in a psychological sense. In the demonstration you convince the prospect that you have the best thing he can use to fill the need uncovered in the approach. In the demonstration you put forth the appeals of your product or service in such a powerful manner that they sink in and sell. And you must make certain that you get the full value and full importance of *all* of the appeals of your product or service, because it is in the demonstration that the sale is actually made. Not in the close, as so many people think. Since the actual convincing is done in the demonstration, this is the point at which the prospect decides to buy (or not to buy). The close is merely a matter of working out the mechanics of delivery. Surprisingly enough, every demonstration produces a sale. Imagine that. Every single demonstration produces a sale. Either you sell the prospect or he sells you the idea that he doesn't need what you're selling. The best salesman always wins.

Most salesmen go into a demonstration in the worst possible way. They unload towards the prospect a barrage of statements all of which represent nothing more than a rapid-fire, unorganized recitation of the benefits and features of the products they sell. They go on and on and on—hoping that at some point throughout this dissertation the prospect says something like—"Stop, I can see how I can use your product so let's write the order." Maybe you don't think this is ridiculous. Maybe you've done it yourself. This would be all the more reason why you wouldn't think it's ridiculous. But let us assume that you had two briefcases. One is a very large briefcase. The other one is quite small. If someone asked you to take the contents of the large briefcase and stuff them into the small one—you would find it extremely difficult if not thoroughly impossible. Well, that's exactly what's happening in that type of presentation made by average salesmen.

Rule number one for a successful demonstration reads as follows: "Fit your proposition into the prospect's business." Don't ask him to fit his business into your proposition. To a prospect his problems are without question the most important things in the universe. Besides, what you're selling is only a small part of his big picture. He buys many other things, which are perhaps bigger and much more important. You touch a very responsive chord in his heart when you appreciate that his business is too big to be unceremoniously and instantly fitted into every proposition that comes along. Furthermore, if you make it apparent to your prospect that you realize that your proposition will be of interest to him only if it helps him achieve the objectives for which he is striving, then you'll have a receptive ear and a prospect who's willing to be sold. During the demonstration you should be astute enough to figure out how your product or service can be used by him and then, in a manner that will be most interesting to him, fit your product or service into his proposition.

The object of the demonstration is to bring the presentation to a routine closing point and to bring it there while maintaining in your prospect a high resolve to buy your product or service. This objective is reached in the least time when the salesman knows enough to keep the interview under his control. Now, this doesn't mean that the salesman should dominate the interview. Dominating an interview is usually offensive to the prospect. However, controlling the interview by guiding it along the lines which best serve the interest of both prospect and salesman is never offensive. This procedure won't irritate the prospect. Also, it takes advantage of the old saying that there are hundreds of followers for every leader. A salesman should always consider himself a leader. He should lead when it comes to controlling an interview. If he leads in a smooth and inoffensive way, he is more often than not able to get buyers to follow his suggestions.

And while controlling the interview and being a leader is essential—doing all of the talking is not. In fact, it's wrong. If at the end of the first 10 or 15 minutes of the interview you are still doing most of the talking, chances are that you are selling poorly. By that time you should both be working together at fitting your *small* proposition into his *big* business. During this convincing process, known as the demonstration, you must at all times speak your prospect's language. Present your appeals in the language which he understands best. Don't force him to translate your terms into those which are most familiar to him. For the most part businessmen fall into three general classifications. There are those who think in terms of *net profit,* those who think only about *gross sales* and those who are easily reached through *prestige.* Whether they are buying for their businesses or for their homes, they are the same individuals and they use the same method of reasoning in making their purchasing decisions.

If you detect that you're talking to someone who is net-profit oriented—then naturally your demonstration should be based on net profits and nothing else. You align your presentation so that it dramatically brings out the net profit that your product or service will realize for the prospect. The same is true of the other two categories. It's a mere case of proper alignment. More specifically— it is a case of using that first, cardinal rule of the demonstration—fitting your proposition into the prospect's business and doing it from the standpoint of what's in it for him. In plain and simple terms: when you're speaking the prospect's language you are zeroing in on his Hot Button.

Assuming that you have a presentation which contains all of the benefits, advantages, features, and appeals, of your proposition—how far do you go in attempting to dramatize your appeals? Dramatize them to the extent that they have impact. By dramatizing you will be able to grasp the imagination of the prospect and he will long remember you and what you said to him. Did you ever hear of Sir Walter Raleigh? Of course you did. So has everybody else. But ask people who he was, and they will be quick to tell you that he was the man who spread his cloak over the mud puddle so that Queen Elizabeth could walk over it. Now, Sir Walter Raleigh had four other claims to distinction all of which were far more important than this dramatic little gesture with the queen. Raleigh was an author, a statesman, a colonist, and a revolutionist. Yet, few have ever heard of him in connection with his other claims to fame. It's the *dramatic* thing that he did which put him in the limelight. It easily grasped the imagination of anyone who heard or read about it.

Build impact into your demonstration by using words and phrases which are strong enough to strengthen the convincing process. When something has impact it brings about action. The right kind of action. Take boxing, for instance. There are two men dancing around in the ring and one is trying to knock the other out. What does the defensive boxer do? He keeps rolling with each punch coming his way. Every time he sees that tremendous, powerful boxing glove coming toward his head, he rolls with the punch. The first time he fails to do so, there is impact—and he gets knocked out. Another example of impact is easily found in baseball. When a baseball player is at the bat he is hoping to make the proper impact when hitting the ball. What happens, however? Home runs are relatively hard to come by. Why? Because if the ball makes contact with the bat at a point just above the fat of the wood, it produces a high fly ball. An easy out. If the contact is made below the fat of the wood, it produces a ground ball, also an easy out. But if the batter meets the ball with a normal swing of his bat, connecting squarely on the fat of the wood—then there is impact and the ball is sent for a long ride. Usually, it's a home run. In selling it's pretty much the same. Throughout the demonstration there must be impact. If your product lends itself to a physical demonstration which is full of impact, then by all means use it. If, on the other hand, you are selling a service where there is no physical demonstration possible, then you must go out of your way to come up with strong words, phrases and sayings which will create the impact for you. The inflection of your voice can produce impact. The way that you produce the impression of impact will often determine just how much of the prospect's imagination you are able to intrigue.

In the process of conducting the Jack Lacy Course we always encourage members of the class to make a presentation. As each man performs before the class he naturally strives for impact. He is graded by the rest of the class so he does his very best. We have seen any number of impactful demonstrations which would intrigue just about any prospect. Salesmen who work for the Scott Paper Company invariably bring in an unusual mechanical device which dramatically tests the strength of paper used for printing, advertising, etc. When a lever is tripped a steel ball, three inches in diameter, drops on a sheet of paper supplied by a competitor and breaks through it. When a similar sheet (of the very same weight and made by Scott) is placed on the holder and the ball is dropped—there is no damage to the paper. Tremendous impact. A clever life insurance salesman produced impact with words. He picked a classmate to act as his prospect at the front of the classroom and quickly asked him a series of questions. He then pointed out to the prospect that the amount of life insurance he owned was just enough to keep his wife and two children out of the poor house for exactly two years. Whereupon he looked the prospect in the eye and said, "You don't expect to stay dead very long, do you?" The entire class laughed. So did the prospect. But before the course was over he bought more life insurance. Guess who sold it to him.

Rule number two of the successful demonstration is: "Classify and simplify your appeals." If you organize your knowledge, you double its value. This has been proved over and over again. If you classify and simplify your appeals to the extent that you'll have them ready for instant use during a demonstration, you will also be able to double their value to you. How do you do this? By taking pencil and paper and writing down all of the functions performed by your proposition. Then, under each function, you list the ramifications of that particular service to the user. By so doing, you will be classifying and simplifying the appeals of your proposition while at the same time making it easier for yourself to come up with them at the right time with the right prospect. Doing this is of tremendous value if you are to follow rule number one without having to search for the right words.

The sequence in which you bring out your appeals in the process of the demonstration is also extremely important. You'll find that one or two appeals always seem to have greater selling power than all of the others. This

being the case, you would be wise to use your most powerful appeals first. Remember, you want to make sales as
quickly as possible. Don't make the mistake of saving
your big guns for the end. We said that in the demonstration you have a big convincing job to do. And the sooner
you are able to do it the sooner you will get to closing the
sale. Use your most powerful ammunition first. You will
probably find, in many instances, that you will not need
the rest of the ammunition because you have accomplished the convincing job that you set out to do at a very
early point in the interview. And the time you saved gives
you more time to make more calls and more sales.

The third, and last rule of the successful demonstration is: "Don't sell your product or service, sell the end
result which it produces." How many times have you
heard the old argument among salesmen regarding tangible and intangible selling? The salesman selling intangi-
bles invariably will claim that if he had a tangible product to sell, his life would be a lot easier. He is certain
that if people can see and touch a product they buy it a
lot quicker. There is a huge fallacy here. People will
always buy the end result a lot faster than they'll buy the
product or service itself. There are billions of light bulbs
sold each year. Nobody wants a light bulb but everyone
wants the light that electric light bulbs produce. People
don't buy something for the sake of owning it. They buy
it for the specific result that it produces for them. This
result may be economy, increased sales, greater prestige,
protection, security, comfort, convenience, healthfulness,
pride of ownership, or any one of scores of other reasons
which help prospects to accomplish their particular aims
or ambitions. To sell impactfully and to convince effi-
ciently, you should constantly keep the prospect in a posi-

tion where he can readily see how he can enjoy the specific advantage resulting from the product or service you sell. This advantage is intangible in nature 99 percent of the time. And this advantage is always related to his Hot Button.

Remember that you have five highways through which you can easily reach the prospect's Hot Button in the demonstration. They are known as the five senses—sight, hearing, smell, touch, and taste. You can't always use them all, obviously, because your product may not have taste or smell. But this is no cause for concern, really, because these two senses are among the weaker ones. So is touch, by the way. (Which blows the theory of the intangible salesman who wishes that his product could be touched, fondled, etc.) A survey has shown that people respond to the senses in the following ratios:

eyes   — 87 percent
ears   — 7 percent
nose   — 3½ percent
touch — 1½ percent
taste — 1 percent

Under these circumstances you should, obviously, concentrate on sight and hearing and take advantage of the 94 percent response they produce.

If you have school children in your family, you probably have asked, at the dinner table, "What did you do in school today?" On occasion the answer was, "We had 'show and tell.' " Each child in the class had to stand up, hold an object in hand, and, while showing it, had to tell something about it. A magnificent exercise. If the average salesman adopted such a technique in his demonstration, he would no longer be average. Why? Take a good, hard look at the results of a survey which was published in *Sales Management* magazine.

|  | After 3 hours he remembers | After 3 days he remembers |
|---|---|---|
| If you TELL something to someone | 70 percent | 10 percent |
| If you SHOW something to someone | 72 percent | 20 percent |
| If you TELL and SHOW at the same time | 85 percent | 65 percent |

Notice that 65 percent figure and the dramatic increase it represents? If you're depending on your voice alone during the demonstration, after three days, you have the 10 percent figure to show for it. When it could be 65 percent. *Show something.* If it can't be the product itself, then show pictures, charts, graphs, reprints, ads, anything. You must make impact through the *eye* as well as the ear.

Notice how attractive the packaging and advertising is for perfumes. They don't rely on the fragrance alone to sell the product. And why do you suppose liquor packaging is so colorful, the decanters so fancy? Because taste alone would never be enough to make impact. The eye must be brought into play.

Never underestimate the power and impact created through the eye. It is more far-reaching than most people realize. There isn't a salesman who hasn't an incident to relate which proves this. One of the most interesting stories comes from my good friend, "Red" Motley, president of Parade Publications in New York. One of the best salesmen in the U.S., Red has made *Parade* magazine, the Sunday supplement, number one in its field. It has the largest circulation and the highest advertising revenue.

Well, one day Red was visiting in his home town in

the mid-west and stopped in to see an old friend, an automobile dealer. In the process of their conversation the dealer said, "Red, you're a famous man, an authority in selling. Maybe you can solve a problem for me. Look at our small showroom—it only holds two cars. Why is it that the car we display on the right side always sells faster than any car we have on the left? It's really strange. If the car on the left has been lingering—we move it to the right and in short order it sells. There must be a reason." Red scratched his head and pondered. Then he said,— "Well, I can tell you one thing that may make the difference. On the wall behind the car on the right side you have a large mirror. That always helps." They shook hands and Red left.

The dealer was intrigued with this observation. So much so, that he spent $250 to have the local university do a research study on the problem. The findings stated that the car on the right side sells faster because,—"when the prospect sits at the wheel and glances at the mirror, he sees himself as his neighbors will see him when he drives up the street in his new car."

It may all sound far-fetched but consider how often you've been exposed to merchandising involving mirrors. Think of the last time you were in a super market. Remember the vegetables neatly placed in their bins? Did you notice the shiny mirrors, at an angle, above the bins? Research has shown that vegetables sell faster when properly lighted and when mirrors enhance their appearance.

The egotism in salesmen fights these facts constantly. I have had, over the years, hundreds of salesmen under my supervision. I've had to work hard at changing attitudes. The toughest, and perhaps the one that shows up most—concerns this very aspect of selling. The salesman boastfully states that he likes to make calls without carrying a briefcase, a catalog or anything else. "I have it all up here," he says, as he points to his head. So he makes demonstrations by merely talking. He's a 7 percenter—when by showing something, he could be a 94 percenter. Invariably, he is a loser. Getting him to build impact into his presentations by showing something is always an uphill battle. Besides being egotistical he's also lazy. He can't be bothered carrying things. When he finally sees the difference in prospect reaction and in sales volume— by showing as well as telling—he admits that he was wrong. But I always think, in these cases, of how many sales have uselessly gone down the drain throughout the country just because sales people love to talk—and do nothing else.

I might add that adopting the *show* and *tell* technique of demonstrating requires finesse. There is a professional method to be followed in showing a product. First of all, handle it delicately. Give it value and importance by the way you handle it. (Much like the jeweler does when he's showing you an expensive ring.) Then, don't just hand it to the prospect. Once he takes it and begins to examine it—you have lost control—to the point that he may no longer hear what you're saying. Instead, you should hold it just far enough away from him that it will seem rude to him to reach over and grab it. And while you're making your points—*look at his face*. (Not what you're showing, you've seen it hundreds of times.) While he's looking at what you're showing, you should be observing his facial expressions. Many times you will be able to spot a particular Hot Button by the very way in which his face reacts at some point along the way.

Having completed this aspect of your demonstration, you can then feel free to let him touch and more closely examine the item. But be sure to get it back into your own hands before you move into the close. You must regain control—and his complete attention—before proceeding with your close.

All that we've said regarding the demonstration is based on the sound principle that it is in this part of the sale that you do the convincing. The more convincing you do in the demonstration, the easier it will be to close the sale. In fact, if your demonstration is impactful and dramatic enough—the close becomes simply a case of working out the details. Never lose sight of this.

A warning, regarding the demonstration, particularly to those who sell technical products. *Don't get too technical.* There is a definite danger in this. Too many salesmen get carried away with the amount of technical knowledge they possess and often lose sales because of this bad habit. Most prospects don't want to know *all* of the technical details. What actually makes it work is not usually most important to them. They want to know what it *will do* for them. The end result is what counts.

Realize, at all times, that if the prospect is knowledgable himself, forcing him to take the "whole dose" will antagonize him. On the other hand, if he isn't technically oriented—and you're talking over his head—he will dislike your superiority. In either case you stand to lose. Why take the chance? If he asks technical questions, by all means supply the answers—briefly and succinctly. But if he doesn't, concentrate only on the end result.

This rule is violated regularly by people who know better. You see it happening all the time. Huge corporations with highly-paid advertising agencies are no exception. One morning my wife asked me to take a pair of her shoes along with me and have the cobbler near the office put new heels on them. After I agreed she threw in the clincher. "Wait for them," she said, "I want to wear them tonight." I told her I had a busy day ahead of me, but this didn't change the picture.

I went to the cobbler before going to the office to get this over with. I told George (who speaks Greek and not English) what I wanted and then asked how long it would take. He said, "You wait here." That still didn't answer my question. As I waited impatiently, I noticed a huge advertisement on his wall by a well-known company. The headline in very bold type, said,

### WHY LADIES HEELS WEAR OUT

I read further:

The average lady has a step of 26 inches. She takes 2,437 steps per mile. Every day that she walks 5 miles, a lady weighing 120 lbs. hammers 731 tons onto her heels. A steel hammer weighing 120 lbs., striking at that rate, would have to be replaced in 3 weeks and would cut a hole a mile deep in 4 months—proving that ladies' heels have a right to wear out. We replace them in 3 minutes.

The last line *finally* answered my question.

I was so intrigued with this violation of the principle *don't get too technical* that I copied it down and had my secretary type it on a note card. When I use it in speeches it brings the house down. It's funny, I'll admit, but also sad. We all know better. Too bad we often go astray— and bring in so much extraneous matter. Matter that really doesn't convince.

In the second part of any sale, the demonstration, the sale is either made or lost. It all depends on you. With impact and common sense you can practice the art of convincing expertly and, more often than not, write up the order.

No one is asking you to become artificial or to change your ways to the extent that you're uncomfortable. Far from it. Be yourself. Use your own methods, your own words and your own ideas. But latch onto the principles in this chapter. Your ability to convince people will be tremendously increased. And that's what selling is all about.

# CHAPTER 6

# THE CLOSE

*There* is probably more misunderstanding about closing sales than about anything else connected with selling. Many salesmen, even after years of selling, still regard the sale as a strenuous tug of war,—at the end of which the prospect signs on the dotted line just as he and the salesman fall over in an exhausted heap. How ridiculous. The close should be the easiest part of a sale. Just how hard or how easy it is, however, will depend on how the salesman has handled the interview. If the convincing process employed during the demonstration is successful, then the closing of a sale becomes almost automatic. It's no longer a question of *if* the prospect is going to buy but rather a question of *how* the actual sale is to be consummated. Obviously, then, one should never move into the close until he is absolutely certain that he has done an effective job of convincing in the demonstration. And, let's not ever assume that the art of convincing is practiced by applying as much pressure as possible.

Let's discuss pressure for a moment. Some people say, "In my business you simply can't use any pressure whatsoever. I'm in an industry where it's strictly the soft sell that pays off." Well, we know that's wrong, because if you don't use *some* pressure, you will get only the easy sales. Other people in sales work will say, "In my business you must use a great deal of pressure. You practically have to hit the prospect over the head in order to make the sale." Now, that's wrong too. You can use so much pressure that you not only lose the sale but you can also lose the prospect forever. He will never let you come back and apply that much pressure on him again. People resent high pressure and avoid being on the receiving end at all cost. So, if you use high pressure you are taking the risk of losing the sale and the customer both at the same time.

The objective of the close is extremely simple. You are trying to do one thing. You are trying to get the prospect to give expression to the decision which he made in the demonstration. The best procedure to use is to make it easier for the prospect to go ahead and say "yes" than it is for him to turn back and say "no." And when you have him in that position, you ask for the order with *expectancy* in your own natural way. That doesn't mean high pressure by any stretch of the imagination. And, high pressure is hard to define, admittedly. What one man thinks is high pressure, another man thinks is low pressure and still another will think it's no pressure at all.

There are two kinds of pressure but they are not necessarily known as high and low. We think that the two kinds of pressure should be known as *offensive* and *acceptable*. Offensive pressure is as unpalatable as poison. This is the kind of pressure which is applied by a salesman who approaches a sale from the standpoint of what he's going to get out of the transaction. If the thought which is uppermost in his mind is the commission (or prestige in his company) which he will gain from making the sale, the pressure which he applies can become offensive in very short order. The prospect resents it. But acceptable pressure is quite different. It's the kind that a salesman uses when the thought which is uppermost in his mind is the sincere and earnest desire to help the prospect achieve what he is trying to do. If in the process of applying acceptable pressure, you keep his Hot Button constantly in mind, your aim should be to satisfy his most dominant desire. Everything else becomes secondary.

Some men are very aggressive and they can ask for just about anything. Others are so timid that they can't even ask for the order. But regardless of which category you may fall into, you *can* be a strong closer because it simply consists of getting the prospect to agree with everything that you have said up to that point in the interview. If you've been successful in doing just that, you have made it much easier for him to say "yes" and go ahead with the closing of the sale than to say "no" and practically contradict himself.

Aside from this very logical theory there is another strategic way in which you can make the close very easy for yourself and the prospect. Avoid the mistake of trying to close all prospects in the very same way. No two people react to a situation in the very same manner. We all agree that people are different, that no two are alike, and yet we quickly forget this when we seem to find a key that

works with two or more prospects. We immediately assume that all prospects can be placed in the same category
when it comes to closing sales. A bigger fallacy doesn't
exist.

You must accept the fact that people think at different
rates of speed. There are fast thinkers, average thinkers,
and slow thinkers. If you question this to any degree and
you need proof, there is a very simple experiment you
can conduct. It will prove to be an eye opener. The next
time you go to the movies and you see a very funny situation developing on the screen, listen carefully to the audience reaction. At a very early point you will hear a few
"hee-hees" here, a few there and a few in the balcony.
These are the fast thinkers who have already figured out
exactly what's going to happen. As the situation becomes
a little clearer, you"ll hear what is known as the roll.
There will be a roll of laughter in one section of the
theater, another roll elsewhere, etc. But, finally, when
the entire situation is completely unfolded on the screen,
universal laughter shakes the walls. Obviously, the slow
thinkers have now caught up. They begin to laugh only
when the funny situation has developed completely.

Throughout each interview, therefore, you should be
constantly trying to determine just what type of thinker
you have on your hands. Once you have arrived at your
conclusion, you will also be able to decide on what type
of close to use when you reach that point in the interview.

The best close to use on fast thinkers is the *automatic
close*. There are two methods through which you can
apply this close:

### 1. Automatic close based on ascending decisions

You first give the prospect something easy to decide
upon and then you proceed with more significant de-

cisions. Gradually, step by step, the rest of the decisions are made as a result of your questions or statements, until the whole transaction has been completed (almost without either one of you realizing what has happened). You simply ask a series of questions calculated to bring a positive "yes" as an answer. The fast thinker follows your reasoning very easily, sees the advantages for himself clearly and agrees to consummate the sale.

2. *Automatic close based on diverting the issue to a minor point*

You direct the prospect's attention to a point regarding your proposition which, though related, has little to do with the sale itself—and you get him to commit himself. For instance. You might say to a store owner, "For each floor display you will get four window streamers. How many window streamers would you like?" If he says, "Twelve window streamers," the sale is closed. No need to talk any further. You write up the order for three floor displays, you thank him and you leave. (You didn't dazzle him with foot work. Remember, he's a fast thinker, he knows exactly what you did—and he went along with you.)

Fast thinkers don't need lengthy explanations. They don't require the spoon feeding you would give to others. So why prolong the interview? In fact, the typical fast thinker doesn't need to be given the whole presentation. Don't insist on giving him the "whole dose."

How do you know, you may ask, when it's time to go into an automatic close? Well, some salesmen have what is known as a sixth sense. They just feel it. Call it what you want, intuition, a feel for people, etc. If you have such sixth sense, you're very fortunate. Accept it and don't question it. But if you don't happen to have it, which is the case with most individuals, there is something you can use in its place. That's known as the *trial close*. You ask the prospect seemingly unimportant questions which take his temperature and tell you how tightly you have him sold. Much like the vacuum cleaner salesman, who, in the middle of his demonstration, stops . . . looks the prospect right in the eye . . . and, says, "Will you be trading in your old vacuum cleaner?" If the answer is, "I certainly will be and you're going to give me a good trade-in allowance for it," then he knows he has a sale. No need to continue the demonstration. On the other hand, if the answer is something like, "Never mind any trade in, what makes you so sure I'm going to buy this vacuum cleaner?"—then he knows that he has a lot more convincing to do and he continues with his demonstration.

As you can see, using trial closes on fast thinkers can greatly cut down the amount of time you spend in making demonstrations. And that's the name of the game. More sales in less time equals greater success.

A big advantage in using the trial close is that it reduces the number of times you have to get the prospect to say "yes" after he has once said "no." Some salesmen (the born egotists), will say, "I don't *start* to sell until the prospect says, 'no.' " If this is their technique and it works, who's going to argue with them? But, it just isn't a good method to follow. Once a prospect has said "no," he now has to contradict himself to say "yes." It makes closing the sale an uphill climb. The trial close is a very good way through which to quickly get the sale closed without the "yes" and "no" factors even becoming a significant part of the closing process.

You must not come to the conclusion, however, that by using automatic closes and trial closes on fast thinkers you can always wrap up a sale in short order. There are obstacles, three human tendencies, which you sometimes must overcome in trying to close a sale. They are:

### 1. Human inertia

Many people are not willing to take immediate, direct action. Perhaps this is the reason why we have so many followers and so few leaders. "We are all as lazy as we dare to be," (Jack Lacy's pet phrase), contains penetrating truth.

### 2. Reluctance to make a decision

As you must have noted, many people postpone making decisions until the last possible moment. They're always wondering if it's the right decision and in the process of wondering, they make no decision at all. Intelligence or fast thinking has nothing to do with this. They understand all the facts, realize all the benefits and know exactly what's in it for them. But to make a decision is the taking of a big step and they live by the theory of "putting things off for the time being."

### 3. Fear of consequences

Many times the prospect will have an inborn fear of the consequences he will suffer if he takes the action you are recommending. He either feels that he shouldn't spend the money at this time, or that he should shop for a better price, or that he might get in trouble with the boss, etc. Your job is clear cut. You have to get his picture of the consequences out of his mind and replace it with your picture of the benefits he will reap. You do this by repeating the end result he will enjoy if he buys your proposition and, naturally, that's always based upon his Hot Button.

In order to properly prepare yourself to cope effectively with these three human tendencies, may I suggest a good exercise. After you have mastered your proposition and know all of the plus factors, sit at your desk with two sheets of blank paper. At the top of one sheet write the words *Hope of Reward.* Then list all of the possible benefits, regardless of how minute, that your proposition will bring to the prospect. Study them all carefully so that you will have them at your fingertips. On the other sheet, place the title *Fear of Penalty.* Here you list all of the consequences he will suffer if he doesn't buy your proposition. The money he is losing by not owning your piece of equipment, for instance—or the time he is wasting which can be converted into dollars, or whatever the situation may be—all fall under this category. If you can narrow these down to a specific number of dollars that he will be losing as time goes on, the urgency of the situation becomes more real. Most people hate to lose money on a continuing basis and will take action to put a stop to this.

Speaking of money, you should also master the techniques of *magnifying the returns and minimizing the cost.* This means exactly what it says. For instance. Suppose you're selling a piece of equipment which will save a company approximately $100 a month. In magnifying the returns, you don't state this figure as $100 a month. Instead, you tell the prospect that it will save him $1200 a year or $6000 in 5 years or $12,000 in 10 years (depending upon the life of the piece of equipment). Such a figure, as you can see, is a lot more impressive than the smaller figure of $100 a month. And, you're not lying. A good salesman never tells a lie. You're simply stating the fact that $100 a month times the number of months the piece of equipment will last will bring him the total of ———.

People react favorably to large savings and they usually lack the imagination to figure out the total savings for themselves.

The technique of minimizing the cost works in much the same way. If you're selling a piece of equipment which costs $350 and will last for at least one year it is much better to say something like, "Would you believe it, Mr. Jones, this machine will cost you less than $1 a day." Here again, no lies are involved. There are 365 days in a year, the machine costs $350, isn't that less than $1 a day? See how simple it is to minimize the cost?

A real estate salesman took the Lacy Course a few years ago and one day stopped in to tell me how successful he had become. I asked him what seemed to help him most. With a big smile he said, "I have become an expert at minimizing the cost." He explained that it is very difficult to upgrade a prospective home buyer. He has a fixed price range in his mind and he is reluctant to look at houses which he feels he cannot afford. "So," he said, "after I've shown him what he thinks he can afford, I then bring him to a more expensive house which I know he will admire. I don't discuss the price until he has looked it over thoroughly and can practically see himself living in it. Then, when he asks the big question, 'How much more expensive is this house than the last one we saw,' I say simply, 'The difference is equal to 2 packages of cigarettes or 1 scotch and soda per day.' After I've said something like that, the price itself never seems to shock him because he's already conditioned his mind to the idea that he *can* afford it."

Now, let's discuss the average thinkers. What types of closes should you use on them? There are two and you can easily become proficient at using both of them. The *dicker close* is very effective because it gives the prospect a choice. Having suggested the action you want him to take, you give him two or more ways through which he can follow your recommendation. For instance. Suppose you are selling a product which can be packaged according to the customer's wishes. Under these circumstances you would say to the prospect, "How would you like these packaged, in 6's or 12's?" You see what's happening? You are actually dickering over *how* the shipment is going to be made, not *if*.

Here's another example. Successful insurance salesmen use the dicker close when they're trying to sell themselves into an interview at the home of the prospect. They first arouse the curiosity of the prospect, then get him to admit that it might be worthwhile to discuss it personally. Then they come up with "Which is better for you, Tuesday evening or Thursday evening?" The prospect is now faced with selecting one night or the other rather than deciding on whether or not an interview should even be granted.

The *pusher close* also has its place. There are many people who simply need a little shove before they will decide on buying something, even though they may really want it. They are actually hoping for someone to encourage them to take the action even if it comes from the salesman himself. In such instances you apply the pusher close by looking the prospect in the eye and saying, "You really ought to buy it *right now* because you can start using it tomorrow (or next week)"—whatever the case may be. "Why delay the start of the money-saving process that this proposition represents to you?" This little shove many times will get you an order from average thinkers who fall in this category. If the proposition you sell requires a signature on the order form, have the pen ready during the pusher close. Hand it to the prospect with a smile and with expectancy. He simply needs that little push even though he hates to admit it.

The *sifter close* is used to sift out the real objection. Because of pride or other reasons, certain prospects don't voice the *real* objection. Instead, they advance a phony objection, hoping that you will accept it and end the interview. However, if you can uncover the real objection, and handle it properly (techniques for this are in the next chapter), you can still close the sale. For instance. If the prospect says, "I would never buy one that costs so much money," he may not really mean it. Sift him out by saying: "If you could buy it for 25 percent less, would this change your mind or would there be some other influencing factor?" If he says, "I'd buy it at a lower price," drop your sights to perhaps the middle of the line and close the sale. If he comes up with another reason—then you've uncovered the *real* objection and you go to work to overcome *it*. Unless you're handling the real objection, all of your efforts towards closing the sale will be fruitless.

There is a special type of close which is reserved for unusual circumstances. It's a close you use on a prospect who, after having listened to your whole story, says, "Now when will you be in this area again?" He's saying "No" in a very polite yet devious way. And with each repeat call the interview ends up in the very same way. He asks you to come back again. He may even give you reasons why he can't take action now but a return invitation is always there. Since most salesmen live to a great degree on hope, they tend to believe this prospect and continue to call on him over and over again. Well, the man who always shakes hands pleasantly as he says, "See me on your next trip," might very well be saying this through force of habit. He never turns salesmen down but he doesn't buy either. He *likes* to have salesmen calling on him. It makes him feel important. The *end-of-the-trail close* is designed for this type of prospect. But I must warn you. A decision has to be made before you can use this close. You, and only you, must decide when you have spent enough time on this prospect. You must evaluate just how much of your selling time he is worth to you. If eventually he's apt to give you *one* order, let's say for $50 to $100, with little chance of repeat business, obviously you wouldn't go back to see him too many times. On the other hand, if you sell a very expensive system for $100,000, with repeat business expected on a regular basis, you would certainly want to come back a number of times in order to try and close this substantial account.

Suppose you decide that a prospect of this type is worth 6 calls and no more. On the sixth call you apply the end-of-the-trail close and here is how it's done. In advance of making the call, write out the order as you think it should be in accordance with the conversations you have had with him on previous calls. Then you confront the prospect with a statement similar to this: "Mr. Jones, either this is a good idea and you ought to sign this order I've prepared for you or it is not a good idea and we ought to forget the whole thing, no longer wasting each other's time." Nervy, isn't it? But do you know what happens? Six out of ten will buy and the other four will turn you down. But you might as well play sudden death and use an end-of-the-trail close in situations of this nature because the four who refused to buy are no great loss. They weren't going to buy no matter how many times you returned. So why not bring the whole thing to a head and go on to other prospects with whom your time may be more fruitful.

For the slow thinker you should use the *picture close*.

With him, because the wheels turn slowly, words don't paint very clear pictures. He can absorb something only if he sees it with his own eyes, and even then, he doesn't want to be rushed. So, always have a pad of paper available and as you make an important point, write it down for him. If you're telling him how he's going to save $20,000, write down this figure in large numerals. It will mean more to him. He will respond to bar graphs, comparisons, isometric drawings, anything that will give him a clearer picture of what you are explaining to him. Many salesmen are afraid to "draw pictures" for fear that they might insult the prospect. Not so. Provided that you have determined, in the course of the interview, that you do have a slow thinker on your hands, drawing pictures will never ruin it for you. In fact, you'll find that he is intrigued by whatever you put down on paper. He'll examine it more than once. It's the fast thinker who will be insulted. As soon as you produce pencil and paper and begin to write, he will quickly say something like, "You don't have to draw pictures for *me*."

So now you have eight different types of closes which you can use in eight different situations depending on the type of prospect you are working with. It would be foolhardy to assume, however, that mastering these closes and the techniques surrounding them is all that is necessary in order to become a great closer. We must not discount the fact that closing the sale is extremely psychological. So psychological that some salesmen, in the anxiety and tension connected with a sales interview, don't even ask for the order. Many may ask once and if they're turned down, they quit. The right mental attitude must be ever present in closing sales. You must be able to keep your head up high, bearing always in mind that what you are doing is nothing to be ashamed of.

Never feel that the prospect is doing you a favor if he buys from you. On the contrary, you must regularly reassure yourself that you are doing *him* a favor because of the benefits which will come his way. Don't ever try to disguise the fact that you are a salesman. Never think that because you are a salesman you are unwelcome. The prospect has absolutely no preconceived ideas about you when you first come on the scene. You're both on equal footing. The only picture which he will have in his mind is the one which you put there by the way you conduct yourself and the presentation you make. If you go to his office in a business-like fashion, and display the attitude that you can do something for him, the prospect will not resent your presence.

One of the worst things you can do, as an example, is to walk into a prospect's home or office and start off with the statement, "I didn't come here to sell you anything." Why dig such a hole for yourself? As soon as it becomes evident that you *are* selling something, you automatically prove to the prospect that you're a hypocrite and a liar. There is no room for either in professional selling.

Don't be afraid of the close. I use the word "afraid" literally. Many salesmen, after making a very fine presentation, never seem to get to the close. They simply keep on talking, hoping that the prospect will *interrupt* and say something like, "OK, I'll buy it." And when this doesn't happen, the interview comes to an end with a handshake while the salesman says, "Thank you very much for your time." This is the easy way out. The salesman didn't put his pride on the line. He avoided the possibility of getting a "no." He was disappointed. And he shuns the unpleasant thought that he didn't earn any money either.

*Ask for the order a minimum of three times.* In fact, *five times* is better still. There is a reason for this. A survey on closing attempts was conducted at Notre Dame University.* This is what the results showed:

46 percent asked for the order once and then quit.
24 percent asked for the order twice.
14 percent asked for the order three times.
12 percent asked for the order four times.

Yet, the very same survey showed that *60 percent of the acceptances* came on the *fifth attempt.*

Do you see now why five times is better? Not until you have asked a fifth time have you given yourself a shot at the 60 percent of those who will say "yes." Naturally, the five different times that you ask for an order would be interspersed with other parts of your presentation. And they wouldn't all necessarily come during the one call either. You could ask for the order three times while you're making the sales call and then write to the prospect a week or 10 days later (there's your fourth attempt) and then phone him a week later, ask if he received the letter and make one more try at closing.

"Ask and you shall receive." You certainly have heard that phrase many times in your lifetime. You've agreed with it. You believe in it. Why don't you adopt it?

Funny thing. People think a lot more of you if you have the courage to ask for something. If you pussyfoot and beat around the bush, they think less of you. Any professional salesman can become a very strong closer. He does this by studying good closing techniques and by training himself to ask for the order at the right time, in the right way and as many as five times.

It's wonderful to have pride and it's great to be every-

* Reported by Dr. G. Herbert True, Department of Marketing.

body's friend. But to bring home the bacon on a regular basis demands that you know how to close. Demands that you have the courage to ask. If there was ever a secret for success—this is it.

# OVERCOMING
# OBJECTIONS

*J ust* when you think that your most convincing demonstration has hit its mark, that you can move towards the
close which you feel is best suited for this type of prospect—what does he do? He comes up with an objection—
one which he seems to have pulled out of thin air. And
now you have a very delicate situation on your hands, so
delicate that it separates the men from the boys in selling.

If you handle the objection properly, you can still make the sale. Handle it poorly—and you can kill the sale, all by yourself. Objections can frequently be a source of a great deal of trouble in selling. But only if the salesman is not equipped with the knowledge required to overcome them in a professional way.

### Keep the customer's viewpoint in mind

One of the major reasons why salesmen find objections difficult to handle is because they keep themselves sold so tightly on their proposition that no one can unsell them. They believe so strongly in the product or service which they sell that the minute an objecion comes up they almost take it personally. They simply won't allow the prospect to say anything that downgrades the proposition in any way. Admittedly this might be considered loyal and most commendable but it works against you. You must at all times remain flexible in your thinking. You must be able to see the prospect's viewpoint and take it in stride.

Basically, the prospect listens to your presentation in one of two frames of mind:

1. Hoping to prove to you that you're wrong.
2. Hoping to prove to you that you're right.

In the latter case, there is obviously no problem. You usually have a sale. But in the former, when he is hoping to prove to you that you're wrong, how you handle his objections will spell the difference.

When an objection comes up, you should handle it immediately, right on the spot. Never say anything like, "We'll get to that later." Or, "You'll change your mind after you've heard the rest of my presentation." Under these circumstances the prospect begins to wonder why you wouldn't answer his objection and for the remainder of your presentation his mind remains cluttered as he tries to speculate what your motives might be. You are not working on an open, clear mind, a mind that can be sold. Besides, the more you make him wait for his answer, the bigger the objection becomes in his mind. It may grow so much that when you *do* answer it, he won't accept your reasoning nearly as readily—if he accepts it at all.

Here's an example of what happens and maybe it hits home. Over breakfast with your wife an argument develops and goes on and on throughout the meal. Tempers flare and a few mean things are said—But nothing gets settled. You leave to cover your territory and, of course, try to dismiss the argument from your mind. When you make your first sales call your prospect turns out to be a most interesting and intriguing individual. The discussion stimulates you. On your next call the customer tells you a funny story and you both have a good laugh. You have already forgotten the big fight you had over breakfast. You go through the day in a most pleasant frame of mind.

Back home, however, your wife is still stewing. As she pushes the vacuum cleaner she says out loud, "How dare he have the nerve to say that to me?" And as the day gets older the argument grows bigger and bigger in her own mind. She can't wait for you to get home. As you waltz into the house, having completely forgotten what went on at breakfast, you greet her with, "Hi, darling." But with her hands on her hips she says, "Don't darling *me!* Now, to take up where we left off this morning . . ." If only you had settled things at breakfast you wouldn't now be faced with a much tougher situation.

Actually, the goal in overcoming objections is to change the prospect's thinking without antagonizing him in any way. This is not easy. To change a person's thinking is a difficult task no matter what the subject matter. But you can accomplish this if you are willing to accept the fact that people tend to build a stone wall around their pet ideas. To break down that wall is a difficult undertaking. And sometimes, it just simply can't be done.

### Facts alone won't convince them

Not too long ago a study was conducted in major New York hospitals to try to determine whether or not it is absolutely necessary to heat a baby's formula before feeding. There was much interest in this study mainly because many infants have a habit of waking up at 2 A.M. and the mothers find it fatiguing to have to spend time at that hour of the night heating the baby's formula. (Besides, the process wakes them up completely—and then they have trouble getting back to sleep.) When the study was completed the results showed that there is absolutely no reason why the formula should be heated—the mother could very easily take a bottle of formula out of the refrigerator, give it to the infant and go right back to bed. There would be no cramps or colic or anything else— and these were proven facts by medical authorities. The study was given widespread publicity. In addition to being published in the medical journals, the wire services picked up the results and the story appeared in newspapers coast to coast. But how many mothers do you really think bought the idea? The majority felt that it would be mean and cruel to give a tiny, little, tender infant a freezing, cold bottle of formula in the middle of the night.

When a radio announcer whose program catered to women in the daytime asked his audience to let him know how many had switched to cold-formula feeding, he was deluged with correspondence. But the ladies didn't say they had switched. They scolded him for even entertaining the idea that they should switch. You see, many times you can have all the proof in the world but if it doesn't coincide with a person's thinking, you have a long, hard road ahead of you.

But this should not be cause for discouragement. Not by any means. People may have strong opinions on certain subjects and breaking this barrier is difficult. But, it *can* be done. Particularly if you follow a simple, two-step formula:

1.  Make the prospect like you.
2.  Try to change his thinking.

If you "soften him up" initially by getting him to like you, the second step becomes a great deal easier. How do you get him to like you? We covered this in Chapter 2 when we discussed the engaging personality. If you follow the rules, you'll find that people will like you in short order. You make it easy for them to like you through your personality. And if they like you—the objections are always minor in nature.

Changing a prospect's thinking also requires skill—the human relations type of skill. When a prospect voices an objection, when his thinking is directly opposed to yours —one of the worst things you can do is to tell him he is wrong. No one likes to hear how wrong he is. Statements like, "Well, that's where you're wrong," or "Let me show you how wrong you are," are suicidal. Why dig such a deep hole for yourself? You had better adopt a strong policy of never telling a prospect that he's wrong. Don't antagonize him. On the other hand, you can't agree with his objection either, you can't tell him he's right and then proceed to show that he is not. That's hypocritical. It may not be quite as antagonizing but it disenchants the prospect. He doesn't like to deal with a hypocrite. You're probably wondering, therefore, which way to turn. You can't tell him he's wrong and you can't tell him he's right. Is there a solution? There certainly is. When the prospect voices an objection, he is usually disagreeing with something you said. He has uttered his opinion on the matter. He's entitled to that opinion. The Constitution gives him a right to have an opinion. Who are we to take it away from him? The best thing to do, and the very first thing to do, is to give him a *decent respect for his opinion.* It's easily done. And here is the statement which you should use to accomplish this very thing. Say to the prospect, "I can understand how you feel, however, . . ." Naturally, there is always a "however." That is a far-reaching statement. You didn't say he was wrong nor did you say he's right. In substance, you said, "Perhaps, if I were in your shoes, I might feel the very same way, however, . . ." And you swing back into your presentation.

Most of the time you will find that all he really wanted was for you to agree that he has a right to his own opinion. Furthermore, by voicing the objection he has given you a clue to what it is, in your presentation, that didn't set well with him. So, as a professional salesman, you go back into the demonstration and do a little more convincing from the standpoint of what's in it for him as it relates to his objecion. You have, thereby, skillfully avoided antagonizing the prospect and yet capitalized on what he said by again going over that part of the demonstration which didn't hit its mark.

Objections fall into three categories, depending upon

their severity. They can be *viewpoints, opinions* or *prejudices* and each must be handled accordingly. The viewpoint doesn't amount to very much. It usually consists of a broad generality which the prospect won't fight too hard for. Generalities like, "New cars cost too much," or "We always stick with our present suppliers," are typical viewpoints. To properly handle a viewpoint, use the following pattern:

1. Give the prospect a decent respect for his viewpoint.
2. Activate his dominant desire by hitting his Hot Button.
3. Swing back into your demonstration and further clarify the point in question.

Most of the time that will be the end of the objection. And if you satisfy him thoroughly, chances are that no more objections will come up in the interview.

The opinion is a more deeply-seated objection. The prospect says, "Your price is too high." He has given this some thought. It is not a generality. He has compared your price with that of one of your competitors and has arrived at the conclusion that yours is higher.

An office machines salesman was faced with this objection regularly. The price of his product was 20 percent higher than his competition. Here is how he handled it. As soon as a price objection came up he would say, "I can understand how you feel, however, there are 2 prices on this machine. The $750 price with which you are now familiar and the $7500 price with which you are not familiar. The latter is the price you are going to pay to be without my machine during the next two years." A powerful answer to the objection. First, he kept the prospect's mind open by giving him a decent respect for his opinion. Second, he hit the prospect's Hot Button by telling him he could cut his operating costs. Third, he carried the prospect's incomplete reasoning through to its conclusion. The prospect had only been concerned with the price. He hadn't thought about the cost to be without the machine. His fourth step was to swing back into his presentation knowing full well that now his prospect had a much more receptive mind.

So, the pattern for handling an opinion is as follows:

1. Give the prospect a decent respect for his opinion.
2. Activate his dominant desire by hitting his Hot Button.
3. Carry his incomplete reasoning through to its conclusion.
4. Swing back into your demonstration.

### Be prepared for common objections

If you find that a particular objection comes up frequently in your interview, build the answer to the objection into your actual presentation. And I suggest that you work it in early enough in the interview so that you avoid its coming up at all. Also, there will be instances where you will be able to sense, from the prospect's reasoning, that an objection is about to be voiced. In such cases, it is best to answer the objection even before it comes out of his mouth. This technique eliminates negative thoughts in the process of the presentation and also impresses the prospect. He marvels at your ability to think quickly enough to anticipate his objections.

Keep a list of the objections that come up in the course of your sales presentations. Record how often they occur and in what order. This will give you an insight as to how many answers to objections you should incorporate in your presentation. Regardless of the product or service you sell, you will find that there will be only three or four objections that come up with any ferquency. Answer those before they come up. But don't bring objections up on your own if they are of the infrequent nature. Why prolong the interview and cloud the issue?

The *prejudices* are the most troublesome of all objections—and they require special handling. These are deep-seated hatreds, loaded with animosity, and they are far from easy to cope with. Here's an example. A customer is promised materials which he needs to manufacture the product he sells. The delivery date is missed by 60 days. When the delivery is finally made, he discovers that the wrong material was sent and he can't use it. The situation costs him a great deal of business. He phones the supplier and gets absolutely no satisfaction. When he finally obtains the proper materials, he is then billed at a higher rate. He's informed that, in the meantime, the price went up. The customer argues that the delay was not his fault but it gets him nowhere. Finally, in complete disgust, he pays the bill as presented but vows that he will never do business with that supplier again. That's how prejudices are born.

Imagine yourself as a brand-new salesman for this supplier. You are very happy about your new job and you are proud to be associated with this great organization. You go out into the territory with tremendous enthusiasm and you call on this past customer without knowing about this incident. What do you suppose the result is? In most cases, the customer is immediately incensed at your very presence. The incident may have taken place a year or two prior to your visit but he hasn't forgotten. He proceeds to tear into you. He recalls the incident in detail, he gets more angry by the minute and you are in for the greatest tongue lashing you ever received.

Coping with such a situation is far from pleasant. It's difficult. But if you use the right formula, time-tested over the years, you can quickly begin the process of overcoming the prejudice.

First of all, you must let him tell you the whole story. Don't interrupt. Hear him out—and sympathize profusely. Agree with him that he was not treated properly. Don't try to defend your company in any way. Allow him to get all of it "off his chest." He has been dying to do this for a long time but he simply didn't have the opportunity or the listener. When he has spent all his fury, has poured his heart out, say something like this: "I can understand how you feel, Mr. Jones. Now, tell me, what do you suggest as a possible remedy for this situation?" At first he will make demands that are far from rational. Yet, after more sympathizing and more discussion, these demands will become fewer and more rational.

Usually you won't get a prejudiced customer to do business with your company again on your very first call. You will find, though, that with each successive call the tongue lashing becomes less severe. And, after a few calls, if you handle him properly, he will begin to like you. His animosity towards your company will begin to take a back seat. When this happens you'll be in a position to show him what you can do for him and make him a customer all over again. He will listen with an open mind only after he has come to the realization that while he's really angry with your company, he's been rather harsh to you, even though it wasn't your fault in the first place.

One thing must be emphasized in the handling of prejudices. In theory, any sale can be made within reason provided that the necessary time and effort is expended in bringing the sale about. However, you are the only person who can determine how much time and effort represents a good investment in overcoming a prejudice. You must determine how important this customer is to you, saleswise. How large an order you are apt to obtain from him and how much repeat business is likely to be yours must be considered. If the initial order and/or the repeat orders are not worth four, five or six calls—then, obviously to expend very much time and effort on this antagonized customer would be unwise. On the other hand, should you decide that he is worth endless effort to overcome the prejudice, it may be wise to make even more than six calls to correct the situation.

Over the years I have encountered hundreds of prejudices. Most of the customers were salvaged. One of the first ones I shall never forget. I had joined a company in the pharmaceutical industry. I was delighted to have made the association and was loaded with enthusiasm. I was assigned a Boston territory and immediately proceeded to "get to know" all of the druggists and doctors that I would be calling on. On the third day I was confronted with a prejudice. Here's the background. Throughout the pharmaceutical industry there has always been a very lenient return-goods policy. When a druggist buys a pharmaceutical product from one of the manufacturers, he has little chance of getting "stuck" with it. If the product doesn't sell, and if he hasn't broken the seal, he may return it to the manufacturer and obtain full credit. The time element involved is not important. Several years after purchase he may still return it for full credit. I was working for a very small company which also had a return-goods policy. But it differed from the rest of the industry. We didn't take *anything* back.

Two years before I was employed the company had merchandised a package "deal" for drug stores. It consisted of an assortment of injectables (liver, B-complex, hormones, etc.) which sold to the druggist for $250. The salesman in that territory at that time had sold one of these deals to a good-sized drug store on the premise that he would obtain turn-over orders from the physicians he called on. (A turn-over order consists of taking an order from a physician and turning it over to the druggist who delivers and bills the doctor, thereby working off the inventory.) At that time, physicians were using injectables to a great extent because similar preparations, orally effective, had not yet been developed. After the deal had been stocked by the druggist, the salesman did nothing about turning the merchandise over. In fact, he never called on the store again. He knew there would be trouble. One year later a new salesman took over the territory and on his first call on the druggist he was read the riot act. He handled the situation easily—he never came back.

After fruitless correspondence with the company, the druggist was seething. For two years he had been looking at $250 worth of injectables on his shelves with absolutely no return on his investment. He had even placed this stock in a glass case to protect it from the dust. When I walked in with a prepared approach, I was able to quickly gain his interest. But, as soon as he realized who I was representing, the fireworks began. He told the whole story with hate in his eyes. I wouldn't dare interrupt. The customers in the store could hear every word. This didn't deter him in the slightest. I could have cheerfully crawled under the ice cream freezer. But I gave him step number one. I sympathized profusely and told him he had been treated very poorly. He said, "No kidding. And you don't look like you're going to do anything about it either. You'll do what your predecessor did. I'll never see you again." In my most sincere tone of voice I promised that I would settle the situation to his satisfaction. That got me nowhere, so I gave him step number two. I asked what he would suggest as a remedy for the whole fiasco. He said, "I'll be delighted to package the whole, ridiculous deal in a box and you can take it with you and leave me your personal check for $250." Well, that seemed most unreasonable, since I hadn't yet earned $250. I then went into step number three. I tried to hit his Hot Button by telling him that it was still not too late for him to realize a very substantial profit on this merchandise, but he said it was probably outdated by this time anyway and most likely worthless. This gave me an opening for step number four. I explained that there was no date on these vials, that there had been no loss in potency, and I went on to extoll the virtues of the products of the company I had recently joined. He listened half-heartedly and his blood pressure returned to an almost normal level. By this time I was able to convince him that he should at least give me the opportunity of seeing the doctors in the area and trying to generate some turn-over orders for him. It was obvious that he didn't believe me as I shook hands and left.

Two days later I returned with two orders totalling $8. You would think that I had sold the entire deal for him. He was ecstatic. He didn't think there was anybody left in the company I worked for who cared about a customer. Every week thereafter I would make it a point to do something for my angered friend. I would not leave the area without generating one or two orders for him, however small. It took almost six months to exhaust the supply that had been there for all that time. In the process, however, we became the best of friends and I obtained some of the largest orders from him that had ever been written in the entire territory. Sometime later we were fishing early one Saturday morning, and as we sat in the boat facing each other, he looked squarely at me and said, "Remember the first day you walked into my store and I practically murdered you?" We both laughed heartily.

Because there will always be human errors which in turn produce prejudices, salesmen must know how to cope with similar situations. While it is true that prejudices are in the minority (greatly outnumbered by viewpoints and opinions) you will nevertheless encounter a significant number of them. Every time we discuss prejudices in a training class the facial reactions of those in attendance are revealing. The pained expressions are proof that every single salesman has, at some time or other, had to contend with a severe case of prejudice. They always seem relieved to learn that there is an answer.

The formula for handling prejudices is as follows:

1.  Listen attentively and sympathize with the customer. Don't interrupt.
2.  Ask the customer to suggest a remedy.
3.  Activate his dominant desire by hitting his Hot Button.
4.  Swing back into your presentation.

The big trick in overcoming objections of all types is to avoid an argument at all cost. You just cannot afford the luxury of losing your temper. It doesn't matter how rude people are to you or how much they antagonize you. There is absolutely no room for arguing in selling. In fact, you must learn to accept blame even when it's not entirely your fault. Use the magic words, "I am awfully sorry." This phrase disarms a prospect. He doesn't hear it very often. His attitude will change, remarkably, because not too many people want you to feel very sorry.

Two of the greatest human virtues practiced by professional salesmen are *patience* and *tolerance*. If you're able to place yourself in the shoes of the other fellow, you will develop the patience necessary to control your temper at all times. Tolerance should come instinctively. We have already said that a salesman must like people. If you like people, you will tolerate them. You will overlook their faults, their odd mannerisms, their eccentricities, and their inadequacies. How nice to be able to say about a person, "We certainly don't see eye to eye but I respect him as a human being."

### Never lose sight of your goal

To a professional salesman an objection, regardless of its severity, never represents a roadblock. In his mind, an objection is nothing more than a temporary detour. He may be slowed down briefly but he immediately categorizes the objection, handles it by using the proper formula and then returns to the convincing job at hand. His presentation continues to flow as if there had been no interruption and his sights are still set on making the sale. There are no hard feelings or negative thoughts. He lets nothing influence his effectiveness.

If you want a rule of thumb to condition yourself in handling objections, try this one: Say to yourself, "I'm not here to win a debate, I'm here to make a sale."

# SALES
# STRATEGIES

$M_{any}$ a war has been won due mainly to the strategy used by the field generals. Many an athletic contest has been won as a result of strategies employed by either the participants or those who have control, such as the coach or manager. In selling the very same is true. Many a sale has been made through the use of strategy—and the salesman who hopes to reach the greatest potential in his particular field or industry must be aware of selling strategies and how to employ them.

*Narrative salesmanship*

The first and most commonly-used strategy is a method called "narrative salesmanship." Practically all salesmen use it, particularly at the start of their career (much of the time without realizing it). Many continue to use it exclusively throughout a lifetime of selling. The most successful salesmen, however, augment it with a mixture of the two higher types of strategic methods of selling. (We'll discuss them in a moment.) The fact that they understand and use sales strategies is one of the reasons they are so successful. Strategies in selling are maneuvers or finesses which the skilled salesman uses either instinctively or as a result of deliberation and thought. When he uses these strategies he gives himself advantages he would never have had without them.

*Narrative salesmanship* consists of direct statements by the salesman concerning his proposition. He weaves these into an interesting—or tiring—story depending either upon his ability to organize his presentation or the interest of the prospect at the time of the presentation. Yet, when a salesman confines his efforts to narrative salesmanship alone, he can do no more than to plunge into a narration of the merits and advantages of his proposition. If he takes the time to plan and organize his presentation, using the 5W's as a pattern, he can, and frequently does, become a good salesman even though he may confine himself strictly to the narrative type of selling.

The advantages to be gained by a salesman, if he trains himself in the use of sales strategies, are unbelievably rewarding—yet it is rare to find a man interested in doing so. Countless salesmen restrict themselves to narrative salesmanship—and they do little more than run off at the mouth. They parade the advantages of the proposition before the prospect in a hit-or-miss fashion—apparently hoping that in some providential manner the conversation will take a turn giving them the chance to make a sale. This is tragic—but nonetheless true. Narrative salesmanship does have its place and if properly organized, gets results. But it doesn't dig deeply. It rarely produces the results possible when salesmanship is supplemented by strategies of a higher caliber.

### Suggestive salesmanship

The second basic method of salesmanship is known as *"suggestive salesmanship."* As its name implies, it comprehends the use of suggestion, a powerful help in selling any product or service. An effective way to use suggestion in your sales work is to master the use of parables. Use parables describing incidents similar to those confronting your prospect and having as their moral the action you wish the prospect to take. If in addition these parables are in the terms of the business in which the prospect is engaged, then you are able to plant an idea in the mind of the prospect more quickly and more clearly than would be possible without such a parable. If you use a parallel situation, one with which the prospect is familiar, you will be making it easier for him to comprehend a new and unfamiliar situation. He will have to exert less mental effort and he can be sold that much more easily. Certainly it is a fact that the things we don't know never occur to any of us. (For instance, for almost 6000 known years, prior to the invention of radio, none of us suspected that the sounds which are now so common were floating around in the *ether*. Or maybe you thought that was an anesthetic.) Furthermore, once you are aware of something, particularly if it is important to you,

chances are you don't forget it too quickly. A baby
crawling on the floor knows nothing of the penalty of
falling. He may crawl right over the doorstep the first
time he comes to it, topple over and hurt himself con-
siderably. But once this happens, the child understands
the principle of the fall, the penalties surrounding it and
it then becomes easy to teach him the danger of falling
from other places. It is much the same in making a sale.
Your ideas must be projected before your prospects and
they must be clear at all times. The best way to be sure
they are clear is to advance them in parallel situations
with which you know the prospects are familiar, using, if
at all possible, terms and incidents related to the prospect's business. When I worked for a pharmaceutical
manufacturer, we were, at one time, detailing physicians
on a certain injectable compound. Its price was high and
this was a major objection. However, over the past several months, there had been much to do about a certain
company's injectables. They were found to contain im-
purities and cause abscesses. During the presentation, I
would hold up an ampule, look the physician in the eye
and say, "Would you believe it, Doctor, it costs us 15
cents to wash and sterilize this ampule before we put anything in it." He knew exactly what I was saying. The possible price objection had been automatically overcome.

Here is another case where we can see this principle
at work. An advertising agency salesman had convinced
an important advertiser, the president of a large company, of the advisability of placing his account with his
agency. (Let's call the president, Mr. A.) There was just
one single obstacle and it asserted itself every time the
salesman tried to close the sale. An advertising agency in
the very same city (operated by a man who had been a
friend of Mr. A's since boyhood), had been handling Mr.

A's account. Obviously, this made the situation difficult. Mr. B, another manufacturer and advertiser also located in the same city, was also doing business with Mr. A's life-long friend. The salesman knew this and he also knew that Mr. B's business was losing ground. The salesman was also aware that Mr. A knew of Mr. B's difficulties. Thus he maneuvered the situation so that all objections were cleared away and then he casually remarked: "Mr. A, two years ago we almost obtained the business of Mr. B, but we could not secure it for the same reason over which you are now hesitating, namely his friendship for this agent. You know Mr. B, do you not?" "Yes indeed," said Mr. A, "I know him very well." And now the salesman drops the remark that is loaded with suggestion. "Mr. A, how is Mr. B's business getting along?" Within ten minutes the deal was closed.

The strategic way in which the salesman subtly pushed the wrong picture of Mr. A's friendship for his agent out of Mr. A's mind allowed him to replace it with the right one. Note how it was done with suggestion—and a parallel situation. No direct statement was ever made by the salesman. It was merely a suggestive technique. Had he brought out the facts directly Mr. A might have objected quite strenuously. While parallels and suggestions are very effective in almost any form, when reduced to sketches or illustrations they become doubly powerful. Therefore, work your presentation out so that it includes parallels and parables for any idea which may be new to any of your prospects. This clarification of your appeals will make it much easier for prospects to see the advantages and to buy from you.

In most instances it is not advisable to issue a direct order or a strong request to a prospect. Most people resent a direct order. (That's why the army sergeant is never popular.) What is your reaction when a salesman *tells* you that you must do a certain thing? Don't you bristle somewhat? We are all alike. The man who does not object to this sort of thing (a direct order from a salesman), is exceptional. Just about everyone likes to make his own decisions. On the other hand, people will run for a psychological or physical gap and try to get through it. This is particularly true if the gap is steadily diminishing. Did you ever park your car in a tight space? Where there was just enough room to get in by maneuvering back and forth between two other cars? And while you were doing so, have you ever had a pedestrian come along and dash through the gap just as the two bumpers were about to meet? It has happened to almost everyone. It's one of the funny little twists of life, of human nature. With the entire block available in which to cross the street, people will actually run for the gap which you are closing and try to get through it before it is too late. They get a slight thrill from this.

During a sales presentation people act in much the same way. While they want to make their own decisions and resent direct orders they *will* run through a gap if you create one for them. Keep drawing closer and closer to the obvious so that there is only one conclusion possible. The one towards which you are working. But never use direct instructions—always use suggestion.

Here is another example. The salesman who is selling a transportation service is well aware that his service costs more than that which the shipper is now using. However, he has a tremendous advantage to offer. His more dependable schedule frequently results in the saving of 24 hours in reaching Chicago from Philadelphia where the plant of the shipper is located. The items being shipped are rubbers for men and boots for women, the demand for which is very urgent during stormy periods. The sales lost during a storm could go to a competitor whose factory is closer to Chicago than is Philadelphia. This salesman has carefully simmered the discussion down to consideration of the advantage of his service to Chicago. Note how he continues to close the gap making it narrower and narrower but still leaving the shipper the privilege of making his own decision. I will repeat only that part of the discussion necessary to illustrate the point: "Does it mean anything to you to save 24 hours on your shipments to Chicago? How much faster can your competitor get his merchandise to the Chicago market than you can? If your warehouse runs out of rubbers during a storm in Chicago, do you lose a great many sales? It's almost vital for you to save 24 hours in getting your rubbers to Chicago, isn't it?" You see, the salesman drew closer and closer to the obvious conclusion with each sentence. Never once, however, making a direct recommendation or usurping in any way the prerogative of the shipper to make his own decision. But the gap was steadily growing smaller and smaller as each sentence— dripping with suggestion of sales lost to the competitor— was uttered by the salesman.

It undoubtedly may require some hard thinking on your part to figure out sentences which will steadily close the gap in your own presentation, but the reward for doing this—and doing it well—will repay you handsomely. Closing the gap is a technique associated with suggestive salesmanship, a strategic way of selling. It will come in handy over and over again.

### Socratic salesmanship

A third basic method of salesmanship and unquestionably the most strategic is known as *Socratic salesmanship*. This type of selling is named after the man who perfected it—Socrates. A Grecian philosopher and sage who lived almost 500 years before Christ, Socrates was the John H. Patterson of his day. He developed a philosophy of salesmanship which has held up through the ages. It is in use today by many of the best producers in all lines of selling. Much as NCR's John H. Patterson left after him a string of men who became famous as a result of having been exposed to his training and his sales philosophy, so Socrates left Plato, Alcibiades, Xenophon and Aristotle. Needless to say, the latter individuals—due to Socratic philosophies—attained world fame.

The Socratic method consisted of questions by which the prospect's thinking was guided to the only correct conclusion possible—the ultimate truth. When Socrates did the selling the prospect did most of the talking, and 'Old Soc' sat back and figured out the reaction as well as the next question to fire at the prospect. He became so good that he rarely missed a sale.

There is no question that one of the most effective things a salesman can do is to train himself in the Socratic method of salesmanship. Ask questions, but make sure they are leading questions which guide the interview so that it will result in a service for the prospect and a sale for you. When you sell this way you benefit from several important advantages:

1.  You pay your prospect a great compliment, you give him a chance to talk about his problems, his aims, his opinions, and his ideas. You endear yourself to every prospect because everyone loves a good listener.
2.  You get an opportunity to think and size up the situation. You will be able to figure out the chief ambition of the prospect, how you can help him

accomplish it, what type of mind he has, what advantages will most appeal to him. This will help you to select intelligently the next question you are going to use in order to bring the presentation closer to the objective towards which you are striving.

3. You learn from everybody. Everyone in a position of any importance in business today has something on the ball and by listening you are constantly learning and acquiring knowledge which will help you in other sales situations.

4. It keeps you out of arguments. It is almost impossible for you to get into an argument unless you express an opinion and it is nearly impossible to express an opinion if you stick to asking questions.

5. You cannot ask intelligent questions of anyone unless you think about their problems and ambitions. When you concentrate on thinking about your prospect's situation, you are automatically training yourself away from thinking about yourself and your specific proposition.

   If you don't think about yourself, you won't talk about yourself—and once you reach that stage, you transform the world in which you live.

As we said in Chapter 1, most of us spend up to 94 percent of our time thinking about ourselves. Therefore, if you train yourself *away* from this you can become nearly 16 times as effective as the average salesmen. Isn't this in itself worth the effort required to master Socratic salesmanship?

Strategies will bring about many sales for a salesman who understands and uses them, sales that would ordinarily never be made without strategic measures. Let's consider a few situations in which sales strategies represent the difference between making and losing the sale. I think you will agree that one of the most difficult prospects to handle is the egotist. This is because such an individual finds it very hard to get his mind off of himself long enough to give consideration to the proposition of the salesman. Well, there are two kinds of egotists. *The first* is the kind of person who has little or nothing on the ball. Yet, to hear him tell it, you would think he's God's gift to the universe. There is not much you can do with this man other than to be as humble as you possibly can and try very hard to find some quality for which you can express an honest appreciation. If you can do this, he will elaborate on it at great length and as he does so you must then try to find a way to get his mind working on *your own* proposition. If you are successful in doing this, you may be able to get through to him. Such men, however, are very hard to sell because making a sale in such instances requires a great deal of patience and perseverance on your part. The time involved may very well not be worth your while. Only you can decide this. Fortunately, not too many individuals in important business positions fall in this category.

The *second type* of egotist, and there are plenty of these, is the man who is good and *knows it*. At least here you have something to work on. One of the best ways to win over this type of prospect is to use reverse salesmanship. You challenge him with a statement such as: "I don't see how you can use my proposition to your advantage." This challenges him to the point that he will set out at once to prove to you that he *can* use it. Apparently he lives in such a continual atmosphere of squeezing blood out of a stone that any challenge of this nature causes him to set out to prove that he *can* do the exceptional thing. Why this is so is hard to explain. But it does work, most of the time. Please remember, however, that reverse salesmanship should only be used when you *know* that your prospect falls in this category. Under any other circumstances reverse salesmanship can backfire on you and literally ruin a sale.

## How reverse salesmanship works

Here is a specific sale which clearly shows how this principle works. This sale was made to a bright sales manager who had 15 supervisors and 175 salesmen reporting to him. The salesman was trying to sell him a correspondence course in salesmanship. As soon as the sales manager realized what the mission of the salesman was he looked at him with withering disdain and asked, "Are you trying to sell me a correspondence course in salesmanship?" To this the salesman courteously answered, "Would it make any difference what it is—if it is honorable and will help you to increase your sales?" "Did you ever hear of 50 cities in 51 days?" asked the sales manager. "Yes," said the salesman. "That was the trip that John Patterson took around the country in which he wrote the sales course which made the National Cash Register Company a gigantic institution." At this point the sales manager then beamed as he said, "I was John H. Patterson's stenographer on that trip. I took all the notes from which that course was written. What could you possibly have in your course that he did not have in his?" "Absolutely nothing," replied the salesman, "but if you could get just one workable idea by reading this course it would repay you, would it not? One idea is worth a great deal to a man in your position but then again maybe you couldn't get any idea out of this course that would be helpful to you." And now the sales manager was off. Down the field he galloped. He sketched his life. He was the secretary to Elbert Gary, the Chicago lawyer, when Gary went to Dayton to work for John Patterson, then he went to several other organizations until he finally found himself in his present position. For several years after he had become their leader, these 190 men had done an outstanding job. However, he admitted that during the past few months "they didn't seem to be clicking." And, as he neared the end of his narrative, he said, "And for the first time in my life, I confess that I do not know which way to turn." The salesman, who had not uttered a word for at least fifteen minutes, knew the prospect had sold himself so he suggested, "Why not turn around and sign this?" And the prospect took his pen and signed the order.

It is very obvious in this case how the use of a specific strategy spelled the difference between making and losing a sale. It became clear at the end of his narrative that the sales manager himself was worried about his problem. He was yearning for help and all that the salesman had to do was to guide the interview in such a way as to start the sales manager thinking along the right lines. As soon as that had been accomplished the prospect sold himself. You can see what would have happened to a salesman using narrative salesmanship with this kind of person. Just as soon as he would have begun extolling the virtues of his course—an argument would have ensued. The strategy known as reverse salesmanship was just enough to start the wheels turning in the proper direction.

### The prospect who won't talk

How do you handle the difficult type of prospect who won't talk? The man who sits and looks at you and says absolutely nothing. He stares at you—but you know full well that his mind is far from the room in which you are in. Or he regularly glances at the correspondence on his desk. Sometimes he just stares out the window. The best way to sell this type of prospect is to ask him a direct question, and then look at him and wait for him to answer. You must remember not to speak again until he answers—no matter what happens. It's sort of a game— the man who speaks first loses. He'll be slightly embarrassed, he'll probably ask you to repeat the question and he'll answer it. But one thing is certain—he'll be listening for the rest of the interview.

A man in Chicago was famous for the way in which he would upset salesmen. He'd sit and look at them without saying a word. He appeared as a monster, yet he was very successful and had been a great salesman himself before becoming president of his company. A young salesman had a proposition which he felt would be quite valuable to the silent one. He prepared himself thoroughly before approaching this prospect and tailor-made his presentation to fit this type of individual. Actually, he condensed his presentation and refined it in such a way that it would wind up with the statement: "There is your problem, this is the solution I suggest—is there any better way that you know of to solve it?" At this point, the salesman and the prospect found themselves silently staring at each other. Neither spoke for what seemed to the salesman to be at least 15 minutes. In reality it was not probably more than one or two minutes. Finally, the prospect broke the ice, outlined a counter proposal, and asked the salesman what he thought of it. The salesman answered, "It's all right, but leaves the problem unsolved. The problem is this . . ." Again he outlined the situation briefly and finished by saying, "Is there a better solution than the one I am suggesting?" The silent monster, who had now been listening intently, realized that none of his solutions were as good as the one the salesman was proposing so he signed the order.

### The ever-present price buyer

On many occasions you have had to handle the prospect—a perennial price cutter—who asks you to cut your price to meet the quotation of a competitor. Prospects who play both ends against the middle by offering you the business if you will meet the cut price are doing themselves and the industry a distinct damage. Here is a good strategy to use on this type of prospect. Suppose he's explained to you that he can buy the *very same* product or service from a competitor at a much lower price. Answer him by saying something like this. "Mr. Jones, you're going to pay too much for that price cut to be safe in using that product. No one in our industry can operate his organization for less than we do. And we could never quote that price without losing money. So, anyone quoting that figure is planning to sacrifice either the service or the product accordingly—or else he will be taking a loss on your business and making it up on you (or someone else) in some other way. If the latter is the case, how can you be sure you have his lowest price? As far as we are concerned, no one will get a better price or a better proposition than we are offering to you. If we have a price decrease, you will immediately know about it. Isn't it important to you to do business with someone who is honest and reliable?"

Most good businessmen don't like to chisel. They respect the prices of responsible sources of supply. However at the same time, they feel duty bound to get as low a price as possible for their own company. Certainly they want to be sure that they're getting the best price in the industry. But when they know they can have implicit faith in the man or company with whom they are doing business, the entire complexion of price cutting changes. Naturally, the price buyer cannot always be overcome through this method. Yet, it will work often enough to be well worth trying. And it is certainly always beneficial to the extent that it places price cutting in its proper light in the eyes of the prospect. You can combat the competition of the uneconomic price cutter with creative selling. Your industry, regardless of its product or service, is in competition with other industries for the consumer's dollar. Therefore, the more money you can get into your own industry, the more business there will be to divide and the less need there will be for price cutting. Whenever you do a job of creative selling by converting someone into a new user in your industry, by selling him your industry, you will find that you will rarely have to bid against a competitor within the industry for that business. Better salesmanship will go a long way towards combating price cutting in any industry. This is particularly true if the industry, as a whole, will undertake to do a job of creative selling. The higher the percentage of any business that is represented by creative salesmanship the less need there will be to compete for business that is controlled or affected by price cutting.

### *The prospect who makes you wait*

When a prospect keeps a salesman waiting he does this for one of two reasons. Either he is actually busy on some other matter that must be finished at once or simply because he has little consideration of the value of the salesman's time. Whichever the case may be the problem of waiting is a serious one for the salesman. Waste of time to a salesman means waste of money. (The average industrial sale call represents an investment of from $30 to $50 for the company employing the salesman.) There *is* a strategic way to handle this situation which will work in practically every case and save you a vast amount of selling time.

Many buyers rationalize that you are "just a salesman" and that it's perfectly all right to let you wait. This is sheer disrespect for your time. When you have waited for a reasonable period of time (10 to 15 minutes—no more) step up to the receptionist or switchboard operator, whatever the case may be, and say: "Will you please tell Mr. Prospect that if I have come at a bad time I'll be glad to return later whenever he will find it convenient." When the prospect receives this word he will either see you quickly or he will send back word as to how long he will be engaged. You can now determine whether to continue to wait or to squeeze in another nearby call or do some telephoning. On the other hand, it may develop that seeing Mr. Prospect today is impossible. In this case, you ask for an appointment for another day. Then, when you come in, you have a powerful statement to make to the receptionist. With a pleasant smile you say, "Would you please tell Mr. Prospect that Jim Smith is here *for his 10 o'clock appointment.*"

Experience has shown that prospects and customers will respect a salesman's time if the salesman respects his own time himself. They will not resent your efforts to conserve it. I have used this strategy hundreds of times and have never irritated any one by so doing. The hours of time it has saved for me are beyond calculation.

I must add at this point that if time must be spent waiting for an important prospect then it should be utilized reading material which will help you to become a better salesman. There are plenty of booklets, pocket-size, not necessarily produced by the Lacy Sales Institute,* which are extremely effective in helping you to remember the things you already know but sometimes forget while selling a prospect.

## Social salesmanship

There are many businesses which entail the use of *social salesmanship,* i.e. entertainment on the golf course, at the baseball game, at the seashore, over the weekend, etc. Naturally, each situation presents its own specific circumstances. Your judgment will tell you how to handle yourself, but as a general rule it is very strategic in such circumstances to say absolutely nothing about the business you are seeking unless your host or guest initiates a discussion. It is much more important to concentrate on being sociable and discussing matters which your prospect prefers to talk about. The prospect is fully aware of your desire to obtain his business and he will admire you and have more respect for you if you don't bluntly capitalize on any social advantage you may have for the moment. Should he initiate the discussion then this changes matters materially and it permits you to discuss a little business. But even then, you should leave closing the actual sale for the office. If he doesn't bring up business, leave it undiscussed. Just before parting, say something along the lines of how pleasant it all was and that you plan to drop in to see him at his office in the near future. In these instances, and, as we have said before, you must bear in mind that people will go out

---

* For booklets and other materials produced by the Lacy Institute please write to Mail Order Department, Lacy Sales Institute, Inc., 80 Union St., Newton Centre, Mass. 02159.

of their way to do business with you if they like you. Using discretion when socializing with prospects is a golden opportunity to get them to like you.

Speaking of using discretion—too often we forget what this word means. Here are a few don'ts which fall in this category:

1. Don't play golf, or any other sport or game, for high stakes. If you happen to win a large sum of money from your prospect or customer, you may have left a bad taste in his mouth. Why do it? He won't like you for it.

2. Don't become a drinking buddy to one of your customers. He may tell you how much he enjoys going out with you to "tie one on." But the next morning, while he will have easily forgotten how silly *he* acted, he will vividly remember *you* in the condition *you* were in. That picture in the mind of your customer will never gain you points.

3. Don't ever go "out on the town" in search of women companions with a prospect or customer. You may be able to prove to him that you're a "fast operator" in fixing him up with a luscious blond. And he'll thank you profusely at the end of the evening. But after that he'll have another name for you—and rightly so.

### New proposition strategy

Whenever the opportunity presents itself, use some strategy in connection with new developments in your line. Before announcing a new product or service, a new model, or a new proposition, ask your prospects and customers what they think of it. It sometimes may be too late to incorporate their ideas but you'll be surprised at how impressed they become over your having considered their opinions. When you later come back to sell them the new development, you'll get a most positive reaction. They almost feel as though they have an ownership interest in it. You'll enjoy the pleasant sales climate.

## On remembering names

It is a distinct advantage in sales work if you can train yourself to remember names. You will agree that when you have just met someone and that person continues to refer to you by your name during that very first interview, you are flattered and you find it very pleasing. To you it indicates that they have an interest in you and your name. (As opposed to the joker who knows you rather well but can never remember your name and greets you with "hi, handsome" or "hi, tiger.")

The strategy of remembering names is not difficult to master. It is just a case of following four simple rules every time you meet someone for the first time:

1. *Understand the name correctly*

    Many people don't pronounce names clearly. Some have complicated or unusual names. It is essential that you understand a name and how it is spelled if you are to remember it. If you don't catch it the first time you hear it—ask the person to repeat it for you. This genuine interest in his name will never offend him. He will not only be happy to repeat it for you—but he'll spell it voluntarily if it's an unusual one.

2. *Say it three times*

    In your conversation with this new acquaintance make sure that you say his name at least three times. Work it into every second or third sentence.

By doing so you are implanting his name in your own mind while, at the same time, pleasing him. You will never meet an individual who doesn't like the sound of his name.

### 3. Associate

As you chat with him, imagine that his name is written across his forehead and try to associate him with some other person or idea. For instance, if he looks like a movie actor, make a mental note of this fact. Such association will help you greatly. (I seemed to have trouble remembering the name of a man who lives at the end of our street. Yet, Jack Hennessey is certainly an easy name. Then I made an association. Now when I see him I think of cognac and Hennessey pops up in my mind instantly.)

### 4. Write it down

As soon as possible, after you've left him, write his name down in your notebook, your records, or wherever you keep items you want to remember. Seeing it on paper helps you even more. Jot down, also, any association you were able to make. Seeing this on paper burns it into your brain more deeply.

Bring these four simple rules into play from now on and you'll be amazed at your increased ability to remember people's names. You won't have to place yourself in the embarrassing position of having to make the age-old statement, "I remember your face but I simply can't recall your name." That's not only a rusty phrase but one that hurts the other person's pride. He likes to think that he's unusual enough for you to easily remember his name whenever you see him. Yes, he has an ego, too.

To be successful in selling you must have a genuine interest in people. We've said that already. You must really like people. Human beings should intrigue you. That being the case, you should *want* to remember their names. Train yourself to do so.

The various strategies we've discussed will all prove helpful—over and over again. But they will never represent substitutes for hard work and mastery of your proposition, two foundations that are vital. Add some of these strategies, however, and your selling power is augmented —substantially.

# ORGANIZATION
# AND IMAGINATION

$D_o$ you like music? Most people do in varying degrees. All of us enjoy it from time to time. Certainly we all know what it is. Yet, if you were asked to describe music in two words—would you be able to do it? Stop right here and think about it for a minute or two. . . .

Don't ponder any longer. It's really easy. Music is nothing more than *organized noise*. It's easy if you have learned to think this way—the way that people think when they have learned to accept the power and importance of organization. Most people know what organization means and they accept it in a matter-of-fact way. But the word, organization, and what it stands for have yet to make an impact on a great many people. They don't realize that without organization you have nothing. With it, you can achieve things that are practically miracles. I never cease to be amazed at what can be accomplished by human beings through skill and organization.

Soon after they had completed the famous arch in St. Louis, I was in that city to interview salesmen for one of our clients. I chatted about the arch with one of these applicants and he told me that they started building from each of the two bases and when they reached the top, the two structures met perfectly. Imagine. The construction plans of this tremendously high structure were so well organized that when they reached the very top from two separate and distinct points of origin—it all turned out perfectly. Before I left the city I had to stare at that arch for a few minutes. It's a most impressive structure—organization made it so.

Certainly you must have marvelled at the technical skill and the organization which was required for the people involved in our space program to land a human being on the moon. But organization can be applied to anything, not just gigantic undertakings. The late Will Rogers was generally credited with being one of the greatest spontaneous wits of his time. One day he walked into a room in the Lamb's Club in New York where friends of his were playing cards. He tried a new, two-line gag on them and no one even smiled. This greatly bothered Will Rogers. He retired to another room in the club where he could be by himself. Four hours later he came out and went back to the table where his friends were still playing cards. He told them the very same gag only this time it was better organized. They laughed so much they were practically rolling on the floor. Would you believe it? Four hours organizing one joke. Was it worth it? It certainly was—to Will Rogers. He used it for many years thereafter and every time he did, he broke people up.

The theory holds true in sports, too. In the great days of boxing, Max Schmeling, with odds of 10 to 1 against him, defeated Joe Louis. Was this a pugilistic miracle? Not at all. Schmeling had made two trips from Germany to America for the sole purpose of seeing Joe Louis perform in two fights. He studied motion pictures of the fights for days at a time. He studied every single action of his opponent. When the day of *his* fight arrived, he stepped into the ring confidently. He had the fight thoroughly organized in his mind. He knew exactly what was going to happen and when. He knew just how he was going to defeat Joe Louis—and he did. There was loads of skill involved, sure, but it was coupled with organization—the likes of which few boxers ever bothered with.

In selling, organization is vital. More often than not it spells the difference between failure and success. Take a good look at a successful salesman, listen to what he says and how he says it, observe his daily schedule and you will quickly realize that here is one of the most organized individuals you have encountered in a long time. On the other hand, think of someone you know who is either a failure in selling or is simply struggling along and you will soon come to the conclusion that his work habits and everything else about him show proof of a definite lack of organization.

There are some salesmen, however, who are not very well organized but who attain a substantial amount of success. They do this by hard work and persistence. When they finally become organized, they suddenly realize how much more successful they are with the same —or even less—effort. Let's take Bill Smith as a typical example. He was a salesman and a rather good one. He knew his product well, he knew the competitive conditions existing in his industry and he had a complete mastery of all of the benefits and features of his proposition. He worked hard and very conscientiously. He faithfully averaged about 36 calls per week. He was able to convert nine of these calls into interviews and every week he made three sales. It took a lot of hard work but he hammered away in a persistent fashion and met with the same amount of success week after week. His sales manager was very happy with him for his creditable job of selling.

Bill didn't think about the future too much. He lived on a week-to-week basis and his major objective was to make at least three sales every single week. After five years of blood, sweat and tears Bill had a long talk with his sales manager. He wanted to know what his future would be with the company. The sales manager said that there was a good future for him but that his sales would have to show a more dramatic increase as each year went by. After giving him a few suggestions as to how he could do this, the sales manager also recommended that he take the Jack Lacy Course. So he sent Bill to the Institute. Well, Bill didn't have a very open mind. Everything we covered in the lectures was not new to him. It stimulated him, sure, but he felt that he knew just about everything that was being said. He watched the films at each of the sessions with tongue in cheek.

After each film he would comment on it—giving examples of techniques which, in his mind, were much better. But halfway through the course something hit him. All of a sudden, he made one big realization—that he wasn't a very organized salesman. How did he come to this conclusion? One statement made during one of the lectures really penetrated: "If you are making as many calls as you possibly can in the course of a week, you have already reached the highest level of your productivity—but if you're willing to organize yourself to make sales faster, you'll have more time to make more calls and get more sales."

Bill took off, jet-propelled. He immediately figured out how he could better organize his presentation, his daily work schedule, his territorial coverage, and everything else about his selling operations. What happened? He completely changed his statistics. He now averaged 72 calls each week which yielded 54 interviews and they in turn produced 27 sales. And this happened week after week. Astounding? Not at all. He didn't work any harder, really, but he knew exactly what was happening at every presentation, organized every sentence to produce the greatest impact in the shortest possible period of time, and because of all this, he changed his averages. Let's take a very careful look at what actually happened:

|  | Calls | Presentations | Sales |
|---|---|---|---|
| Former average | 36 | 9 | 3 |
| Present average | 72 | 54 | 27 |

Note how he was able to double the number of calls made each week. Note, too, that instead of doubling the number of presentations he was able to make 6 times as many presentations. And most important of all—instead of doubling his sales, he is making 9 times as many sales as he ever did before.

Now these ratios of calls, presentations and sales may not apply to your particular industry or to the product or service which you sell. But the principle does. The figures are incidental. The principle, however, as it applies to your work in selling, is vital. It will pay you tremendous returns if you always keep in mind that:

THE LENGTH OF TIME IT TAKES YOU TO MAKE A SALE DETERMINES THE DEGREE OF YOUR SUCCESS AS A SALESMAN.

### Improving your salesmanship through organization

That you can improve the quality of your salesmanship through organization is an accepted fact. The question is, however, exactly how can you do this. There are three things that you, as a salesman, can organize:

1. Your knowledge
2. Your personality
3. Your work

To attain the greatest measure of success in selling all three of these elements must be completely organized and they must mesh and synchronize with each other.

By organizing your knowledge you will be able to make presentations to all types of individuals in the quickest and most impressive way. Assuming that you know all that there is to know about your proposition, you need simply to follow the 5 W's which were thoroughly covered earlier in this book. Then—and only then—will you be able to make a presentation which touches all the bases in the right sequence. You leave absolutely nothing to chance and you are fully insured against a prospect or customer who doesn't get your message simply because it doesn't come across in a manner which he can understand.

Organizing your personality makes it possible for you to become much more effective with more people. The impression which you make on others is always governed by your personality and, as we have already said, if people like you, they go out of their way to do business with you. If you want them to believe you and accept your recommendations, the interview must go beyond the point of the first impression. If it docs, and your personality has done its job for you, more sales will keep coming your way. Chapter two thoroughly covered the subject of personality and I suggest that you review it periodically. It's so easy for all of us to slip into bad habits every so often—habits which affect our personality. It's a human tendency. The only way to make sure that our personalities remain sales oriented and thoroughly organized is to review the rules that we must follow constantly to keep ourselves on the right track.

By organizing your work you will be able to get the maximum value from the time and effort which you expend in the actual mechanics of your sales job. If you can get the details of your work so well organized that you can get things done in the quickest way with the least amount of work, then you will obviously be getting maximum sales in a minimum of time. Many salesmen are said to be constantly "spinning their wheels." Their work habits are so disorganized that to get things done takes them two, three or even four times as much effort (and time) than it takes a man in the same industry who *is* organized.

Evidence of this is available just about any day that you care to research the situation. All you have to do is stop in at a roadside diner, coffee shop, etc. between 10 and 10:30 on *any* weekday morning. You will marvel at the number of salesmen who are there, sitting down very leisurely with a cup of coffee and perhaps a donut, and thumbing through a little notebook listing all of their customers and prospects in their territories. Know what they're doing? *They are trying to decide where to go for the day.* Shocking, isn't it? These are full-grown men who know better. They probably did nothing significantly important the evening before. They didn't get up too early that morning, had a hearty breakfast and left the house about 9 A.M. (when they should already be making that first call). They probably did a few errands before getting on territory, and then decided to stop somewhere, have coffee and finally to determine where the day should bring them. Under these circumstances, that first call probably won't be made until 11 A.M. And then they talk about "bankers' hours." Nowadays the banks open at 8 and close around 5 with additional hours a couple of evenings a week and some Saturday mornings thrown in. Many salesmen aren't on territory more than four or five hours a day.

### Learn to budget your time

As you can readily see, one of the most important things a salesman should do, organizationally, is to *know where he is going* every day when he leaves his house to cover his territory. Not only should he know this the night before for the following day—but he should know where he's going every day for *one month* in advance. In other words, he should have an itinerary for 30 days. Some companies require such an itinerary. They insist that the salesmen submit one for approval. The amount of approval is usually minimal but in having such a rule they force the salesmen to sit down and write out an itinerary. If your company doesn't have an itinerary policy—you should place such a requirement on yourself. Only then can you be thoroughly organized regarding territorial coverage. You can argue that having an itinerary will many times seem ridiculous. Certain things that come up on territory may force you to go to a town other than the scheduled one because of adjustments, price changes, or other factors. OK, there *will* be changes to your itinerary and for legitimate reasons. But at least you *do have* an itinerary, you *do have* a plan. The changes will upset it to a degree but you can always get back on the track. Or you can substitute your scheduled day in this town for one day in that town in adjusting for the change. The point is—without an itinerary many irregularities can be noted in a salesman's territorial operation. Perhaps the most significant is that he will tend to call on active accounts much more often than is necessary. This automatically produces almost a complete neglect of prospective accounts—a sad mistake in any salesman's operation. If your itinerary brings you to town A, some 50 miles away from any other town, and you only have 3 customers in that town, you will then find it necessary to call on the prospective customers as well because you are scheduled to stay in that town for the day. It is a system that makes it easier for you to do the things you should—the things that many of us let slide by.

There are a host of other ways in which you can organize your work. The itinerary obviously applies to *everyone* in outside selling. Additional ideas which we will now discuss will not necessarily apply to every salesman because of the varying natures of different industries—and, in some cases, the varying aspects of territories within the very same industry. However, we will set forth these organizational ideas and you can select from them those which you feel apply to your particular situation. Some of them may have to be revamped or adjusted in some way to fit your specific needs. Feel free to do so. You should be concerned with the underlying principles of these organizational systems—not the details. Don't discount any of them because they don't apply directly.

### The importance of records

I'm sure that you will agree that any system of organization for a salesman should be geared to reducing paper work to an absolute minimum. Salesmen, in general, hate paper work, and record keeping—yet companies force them to do more and more of it as time goes on. A certain amount of record keeping simply has to be done. Here are some ways in which to keep it simple:

### The record card which condenses all information

This is a must. Start a card file today, if you don't already have one. Don't wait for cards to be printed or for any other reason to delay this organizational tool. The size of the card is not important. If you can put everything we're going to suggest on a 3 x 5 card, fine. If not, get a supply of larger ones. At the top of this card you place the name and address of the customer or prospect, the name of the buyer, etc. Then use a portion of the card to record by months, or weeks (whatever the situation may be) the calls you have made and how much business this account has given you. Naturally, these figures will, at a glance, tell you whether you are gaining or losing ground with the customer. And this is information which you can use, since one of the worst things you can do during an interview is to actually ask the customer how much business he has been giving you. He will expect you to know. On the very same card you should record any other pertinent information that might help you in servicing this account. (Or opening this account, if it is a prospect.) Information such as his hobbies, his opinions on interesting subjects, how many children he has, their names, the date of his birthday or his wedding anniversary and just about anything else that will enable you to strengthen your personal relationship with him.

Have these cards in some sort of box *right in your car.* (We designed and produced a Car Desk for this very purpose and have thereby increased sales for thousands of salesmen.) If you keep the cards at home hoping to transfer information to them—I can guarantee you, it won't work. In your car, you'll be jotting down important tidbits on these cards immediately after a call. Also, just prior to making the call, you can refer to the card and remind yourself of any important information regarding this customer or his operation (certainly his Hot Buttons). When you walk in armed with the information which you just reviewed on his card, you will invariably impress the prospect or customer. He assumes that you have it all in your head. You'll stand out—far above Mr. Average salesman who goes in floundering, not even remembering how long it was since his last call. He doesn't know very much about what's going on with this account and plays the whole thing *by ear.* If you get yourself well organized, you don't have to play anything by ear. You do things in a more direct and productive way. Incidentally, file these record cards geographically by states, cities or even streets. The reason for this is so that when you are making a call in a particular town in your territory you can immediately determine who else is nearby. This insures that you make the best possible use of time wherever you happen to be.

*A reminder file which never lets you forget* is very easy to set up. You do this with ordinary filing folders. Mark one folder for each working day of the week and also one folder for each month of the year. (Some 35 folders in all). Place them in a box with the monthly folder first and the day folders following it. Whenever you have something to remember, you merely drop it into the folder of the day on which you want to do something about it. If it's something which doesn't need action for a few months, you simply drop it into the folder for the month involved. At the start of each month you simply distribute the items in the monthly folder to their proper days in the forthcoming month. Each evening you pull out the folder for the following day and you are quickly reminded of what needs to be done. If the item to be looked after doesn't coincide with your itinerary, you simply refile it in your reminder file in accordance with your itinerary. If a phone call is necessary to rearrange the scheduling with the customer or prospect, make a note of this so you won't forget.

You will be most pleasantly surprised at how this system will yield big returns for you. Before very long you will be astounding the people you do business with. They'll think you have a supernatural memory because they are accustomed to having salesmen tell them that they either forgot something or they throw in a little white lie as to why it couldn't be done on time.

If you have phone calls to make in lining up appointments or business, list them on a 3 × 5 card the night before. Keep the card in your coat or shirt pocket and, on the next day, make the calls in order of their importance at strategic times during the day. Strategic from the standpoint that they should not all be made at one time thereby sacrificing the time for a sales call. There is always a period in each day when you can make calls. For instance, if you know that you have to wait ten minutes to see a prospect or a customer, why not make one or two calls during that time? Some salesmen spend half the morning on the telephone only to discover they didn't reach too many of the people they tried to get—a great way to cause a dip in the sales curve.

Now let's talk about daily reports, a very sore point in the minds of some salesmen. Perhaps your company already requires you to make out a daily or weekly report. And if they do, it is very likely a complicated report with which you hate to contend. In fact, you probably put off filling it out until you absolutely have to. This is understandable. Paper work has always burdened the salesman and it probably always will. However, nothing, and I mean absolutely nothing, can give you a clearer picture of what you have accomplished than the filling out of a daily or weekly report. A salesman can easily become enthused over promised sales but if they never materialize, he really doesn't have anything to show for his efforts. Some companies have given up daily reports. They feel that the time involved does not justify the information gained. However, if the orders don't come in as often as expected, the very same companies begin to question the salesman on whether or not he has been covering his territory.

If you are already in selling and your company requires a daily or weekly report, you should have this handy in your car so that you can fill it out as you go along. It only takes a few minutes after each call. You can only retain details for so long. So it's a good idea to fill out the form while everything is fresh in your mind. It should actually become automatic with you, this routine of immediately jotting down exactly who you saw and what you talked about so that it becomes part of your selling routine. Even if your company does not require such forms to be filled out by you, the routine is so helpful that you should develop a report form of your own. It will give you at a glance an excellent idea of how well you're doing. As they accumulate you'll be preparing a perfect file to which you will refer much more often than you realize.

All of us need motivation of some sort. There is no better motivation for a salesman than to look over a daily or weekly call report sheet and realize that he hasn't sold one-tenth of his quota for that period. Such a realization makes you fight a lot harder for every piece of business that you think should be yours. It makes you see clearly that while you may have had many promises you still don't have the sales to show for your efforts. The adrenalin begins to flow. You *do* something about it.

A daily report need not be a complicated thing. You really only need four columns: one for the name of the company you called on; the second for the name of the individual and his title; and the third (and this should be the largest) for "discussion held." In the third column you list all of the things that you talked about, what the possible outcome of the call will be and whether or not you got an order. The last and fourth column is for dollar volume of order taken.

Have a supply of these mimeographed and then be very religious about using them. At the end of each month you can total the number of calls you made, how many of them turned into orders and find the total dollar volume of your orders. This recap will become very valuable to you. However, don't make the mistake that many people do. They list all the calls they made whether or not they were able to see the individual who does the buying. This is a great way to kid yourself. You call on the ABC Company and you ask for Mr. Jones only to discover that he is on vacation—if no one else can help you but Mr. Jones, you *didn't make a call*. Some people argue that it was a call but it didn't turn into an interview. You can argue about semantics all you want. The fact is that having stopped at the ABC Company produced absolutely nothing. At best it produced an appointment to see the buyer when he returns from his vacation. To list it on your daily report is ridiculous because it doesn't prove a thing. You will be inflating your ego by adding to the number of calls you make, but you're only playing games with yourself and defeating the purpose of the whole idea. You're trying to motivate yourself into doing as good a selling job as you possibly can. To do so you must keep a daily report sheet that reflects the true picture of your accomplishments. Only then will it stimulate you into doing even more—and doing it better.

### Developing imagination as a sales aid

Very closely allied to the subject, organization, is the mental faculty known as *imagination*. I'm sure you've met many people who very freely admit that they do not have any imagination. This is perhaps one of the major reasons why real estate salesmen always try to show a house while the present owner is still living in it. The prospective owner, under those circumstances, doesn't necessarily have to use too much of his imagination because he can readily see how comfortable the home can be and how much furniture it will hold. On the other hand, if he were showing the very same house after it had been emptied of its furniture, the unimaginative prospective buyer would find it difficult to picture his own furniture in it. An empty room would seem altogether too small for him. "The king-size bed will never fit in this room," he would say to the salesman. But, if he's looking at the room with such a bed already in it, he can easily relate and see the possibilities.

However, no one should deduce from this that you either have imagination or you don't. It's true that some people are gifted with a tremendous amount of imagination. Yet, those who are not, can certainly develop a great deal of it if they make an effort to do so. In selling, as in almost anything else, imagination can help tremendously in making you much more successful. Many, many times it can spell the difference between making the sale or losing it. Particularly if the salesman is working with a prospect who doesn't have much imagination of his own. Yet, it should also be noted that imagination can also be a dangerous thing. Under control, it is one of the most powerful forces which a salesman can use. Out of control, it becomes one of the most destructive forces with which a salesman must contend.

Did you ever give much thought to what imagination really is? Here's a simplified definition: imagination is the mental faculty through which we *create* or *conceive* *images*. These are *new* images as opposed to the recalling of old images. By images we mean every thought, word, deed, concept, idea or impression of any kind.

The memory, which meshes with the imagination, is the mental storehouse in which we keep our old images. They are easily recalled and that's why so many people think they're being imaginative when they really are not.

They pluck out an old idea, reuse it exactly as it was used before, and then pat themselves on the back for being so imaginative.

The will, which also must enter into a discussion of this nature, is the mental power through which we control our acts and thoughts during our conscious hours. Nothing ever happens unless the will of a human being has played its individual role.

Memory, imagination and the will are so interwoven and so completely synchronized that, given a familiar situation, all three faculties will function with split-second timing. For instance, when you're driving along a highway and the rear lights of the car you're following brighten up, what do you do? You instinctively apply your own brakes. Why? Because you remember, from past experiences, that unless you do so you may get into a bad accident. All this is stored in your memory, your subconscious mind, and it only takes a fraction of a second for you to recall it.

Did you know that your subconscious mind works all of the time whether you are conscious or unconscious and that it works with the speed of lightening? It's a marvelous mechanism and one that we should take advantage of more often. There are two ways through which you can get ideas or images into your subconscious mind. You can do so via the senses. Anything you experience with any of your five senses leaves an image in your memory or subconscious mind. These are called sensory images. The other way is through your imagination. This avenue is a little harder. It requires mental effort and this, for many people, is analogous to hard work. To think consciously about new ideas and develop them to the point that they can be used successfully for what we are trying to do, is not easy. Deep thinking is necessary. However, it pays big dividends because images which we place or store into our subconscious minds are easily recalled whenever we need them. And, like everything else, what is easily acquired is never as valuable as what must be worked for. The sensory images—easily acquired (and stored)—certainly have value. But the imaginative images—harder to acquire, yet just as easily stored— usually have much more value.

There is little question that imagination, under control, is the greatest force in the world. Through it we have gained many things, like the airplane, the radio, the automobile. Every single invention represents an imaginative effort by someone willing to conceive, and follow up on, imaginative images. If it were not for imagination, we would most likely still be living in caves. Yes, imagination dictates every voluntary act of our lives. Before any of us can do anything we must first imagine ourselves doing it. Out of control, however, the imagination leads people to commit rash, unreasonable acts. Well-planned robberies or murders are examples.

Every single achievement, including your sales, takes place in the imagination of someone's mind before it becomes an actuality. If the sale doesn't take place in your own imagination before it is made, then it certainly must take place in the imagination of the prospect. Now, you can always do something about activating your own imagination but you have little control over the imagination of the prospect. Oh, I suppose you can influence his imagination in many ways by leading him down the path, step by step, but why take this long, hard road? Why not complete the sale in your own imagination in advance? Do this before you make the call. Plan and go through the entire interview in your own mind. Then, when you're actually engaged with the prospect, you will be on ground that's familiar to you. Far from being strange it will seem familiar—because you've already been there through the help of your imagination.

When we are confronted with an unfamiliar situation we work slowly often reaching into our memory for something similar to use as a guide. Then we depend on our imagination to develop an image of what we should do— all of which takes time. This is why a salesman, encountering unfamiliar situations during interviews, is slowed down so much that he frequently loses the sale. But if the situation is very familiar to him (having experienced it in the past or having imagined his way through it), he forges ahead with confidence, doesn't have to stop and ponder, and is able to be much more convincing.

To be successful in selling you should learn how to give your imagination an almost daily workout. It's much the same as developing a muscle. Every single day you should think of new and different ways of doing your routine chores. You should ask yourself, over and over again, "How can I do what I'm doing *differently and better?*" This is the type of thinking that develops your imagination. And since selling, in many ways, represents a distinct challenge, the challenge of second guessing the prospect, you should constantly bring into focus bizarre situations which have not happened but certainly could during any particular sales presentation.

Here is an example. Perhaps basic, but most likely one which will make you realize how little we think about very plausible situations. Nowadays it is almost unheard of for a salesman to be literally thrown out. We are a civilized nation and, by and large, we are rather polite to each other. While a salesman might be told that he's calling at a bad time or that inventories are high—the fact is he's never told to "get out" in so many terms.

Have you ever thought about this? Have you ever thought about what you would say if it happened to you? Would you simply turn around and leave feeling totally rejected? Would you rationalize that you didn't need the business of such a rude person? Would you try to save the time and effort you expended in making the call by attempting to remedy the situation? This is what we mean by being ready to cope with an unfamiliar situation. Since this doesn't happen to you very often, if at all, you're not fully prepared to cope with it. Rather than being stunned and rendered speechless—wouldn't it be better to be ready with some sort of retort which might still get the person's interest—and pave the way for a possible sale?

I suppose the real reason why most people don't develop an active imagination is because they don't fully realize how powerful and impactful it is to have one. They never stop to think about it long enough to make the realization. Let's work on that for a moment.

Any professional comedian will tell you that the most successful jokes or stories, that produce spontaneous and prolonged laughter, are those which capitalize on the element of surprise. The punch line or ending has an unexpected twist. The vast majority of the listeners are not able to anticipate the comedian. Why? Because the vast majority lacks an active imagination. Even the few that do have one can rarely put it into play fast enough to figure out what's coming next.

The same can be said of successful novels or murder mysteries. A master in the latter category has to be Alfred Hitchcock. His works consistently astound you. The endings are always beyond your wildest expectations. And that's precisely why he's been so successful. He has a wild, rampant imagination. He knows that most people don't —and he capitalizes on this.

Still another example may bring this point closer to home. We are living in an age of traffic tie-ups. With most of us it's rush-hour routine to listen to traffic reports on the car radio broadcast by a helicopter overhead. And there's nothing more exasperating than to be inching along at 2 miles an hour on a freeway where the speed limit is 70. Yet most people complain, sigh and even cuss instead of figuring out an alternate route. That takes imagination. I had a chat recently with an interesting pilot who works for a radio station and airs the traffic reports. He told me how disappointed he was in the human mind. If he gives alternate routes to circumvent tie-ups—motorists will take them. If he doesn't—they do nothing. He said,—"Imagine how many important people with responsible jobs are driving those cars—and yet I have to tell them to turn on their headlights at dusk. As I do—all the lights go on. I feel good about it, because it shows how many of them are tuned to our station. But really, if you think about it, they just don't stop to figure things out for themselves. I've had to tell them to turn on their headlights in heavy fog just before being grounded myself. Wouldn't you think they'd come up with such a safety precaution all by themselves?"

You shouldn't be too surprised at this human failing— if you are, you are proving, at the same time, that you haven't been very observant. Do you know why people riding motorcycles wear helmets? Because most states passed a law making this compulsory—*not* because the cyclist used his imagination. And, in case you want to write that example off as one which involves only the younger generation—how about the automobile manufacturers? It took Ralph Nader and federal intervention to get them to install safety features in the cars they make. The same imaginative talent that comes up with a new model each year could have been put to work in the safety area long ago. Why wasn't it? Because the highly paid top executives in that industry are no different than those in any other industry. They either lack or don't exercise their imagination.

There is no need to give you more examples for you will see for yourself now that you are more aware. You will see clearly how few are the people who have the imaginative ability to see the advantages and benefits of the product or service you sell. They may listen, but the mind is not automatically recognizing their need for what you're selling. You have to do it for them. So, if you want insurance for success, you had better decide right now that you will develop and constantly use your imagination. Then, on the rare occasion when the prospect also displays an imagination—you'll close faster and make a bigger sale. It will feel much like hitting the jack-pot with a slot machine. Delightful—but rare.

# ANALYSIS AND CHECK UP

**O**n various occasions throughout this book you have noted, I am sure, the repeated use of the term, *professional salesman.* I hope that, by this time, there is no question in your mind that the successful salesman must be a professional. Many who are not in selling may argue this point with you. They'll insist that the professional is an individual who practices a profession such as law, dentistry, or medicine. This generalization is made for good reason. It is assumed that what made these people professionals is the vast amount of education and training

169

that was necessary to qualify them for their positions in today's society. Salesmen, on the other hand, don't ordinarily receive too much training. Therefore the public will ask, "how could they be professionals?"

Well, it's all a matter of attitude. Anybody can become a professional in his field if he cares to do so. A salesman is no exception. If he strives to better himself, on a continuing basis, he will become a professional. You, for instance, have taken a giant step by reading this book (and possibly for some of you reading it over many times will mean an even greater payoff). You want to become better in the field of salesmanship. You want to do more than just talk to people when making a sales call. You feel that for the salesman the making of a sale is no different than the treatment of a patient is for the physician. You are quite right.

### Learning to analyze

When the physician uses his stethoscope, or X-rays or any other diagnostic means, he is trying to determine exactly what the cause of the ailment may be. He does a very thorough job of analyzing the situation before he even considers the prescribing of a remedy. The professional salesman operates in much the same way. Every time he comes face to face with a prospect or customer he thoroughly analyzes the problems, needs and desires of this individual and then proceeds to fit his proposition into the prospect's business. He becomes a master at listening. An expert in human relations. And when he has a very clear picture of the situation at hand, he is able to make recommendations much like the physician prescribes the medications.

In so doing he makes absolutely certain that he speaks

the prospect's language. He must be a communicator of the first order. This requires being on the same wave length as the prospect is throughout the entire interview. In the close, it requires a reiteration of the benefits in accordance with the way in which the prospect thinks about his business problem. In this regard, most business-men fall into one of four groups:

1. Net profit minded      3. Prestige minded
2. Gross volume minded     4. Idealistic

Suppose you were selling the president of a company, a man who you have decided is prestige minded. A state-ment like, "Can you see how this service will add to the prestige of your company?" will be very meaningful to him. On the other hand, if you were talking to a treasurer who is usually net profit minded, you would most likely say something like, "Installing this system will greatly increase your net profits." And so it goes, you speak to them in terms which they understand in accordance with the ways in which their thinking is channelled.

Cultivate the habit of analysis. Make it a practice to analyze everything and everybody. With an analytical mind you can stay one or two steps ahead of almost any-body else. This helps tremendously in sales work. How-ever, make certain that when you analyze people you do so from a constructive standpoint only. Look for their good points. It's very easy to be destructive and single out the bad points—that gets you nowhere. You must also analyze yourself and this too must be done constructively. Don't approach it by asking what might be wrong with you. Instead, ask yourself what you can do to make yourself better, saleswise. Latch on to that word, "better." All of us can become better at what we do. There is no end to improvement. Many people find self-analysis a very simple matter—they just sit back and feel completely satisfied with themselves. In the process of being overly constructive, they pat themselves on the backs incessantly. Herein lies the answer to why so few salesmen are really professionals. This self-satisfaction born of egotism convinces the individual that there's no need to take any specific action to improve his selling skills. As soon as he has made a few sales he considers himself a super salesman. How unfortunate.

Our experience over the years in training salesmen has clearly revealed that most salesmen are outright egotists. Because of this they don't exactly know what they're doing. Now that sounds like a very ridiculous statement. You'd think that if a man is making a living, and in some instances a very good living, he certainly must know what he's doing. What we mean is that if you were to ask one of these men questions like, "What are the three parts of any sale, which is the most important, etc." he quickly would flunk the test. And you will have to admit that that falls in the category of not knowing exactly what he's doing. He has never stopped to figure out how he could improve his method of selling and, therefore, never carefully examined exactly what happens on each sales call.

About two years ago something unusual happened in the very last session of one of the Jack Lacy Courses which we conduct. It was graduation night and almost time to pass out the diplomas. A member of the class, a man in his early 60's, asked me if he could say something from the podium. Naturally, his request was granted. We always encourage enthusiasm of this nature. With a stern look on his face he began to expound. He said,—"I want all of you to know that throughout this entire course I haven't learned one single thing that I didn't already know." I cringed. It was the first time this had ever happened. "But," he continued, "I also want you all to know that it took me 40 years to learn it all. You younger men have had the opportunity of learning what selling is all about without going through the many years of trial and error that I had to experience. When you are my age every single one of you will have earned much more money because this knowledge was made available to you in such simple and interesting terms. In fact, if you use it religiously, you'll all be rich, which I'm not. I didn't have your head start."

Funny thing, though—he was one of the most enthusiastic men in that class. He participated constantly and asked many questions. He loved every minute of it. When I later asked him about this he admitted that his enthusiasm was due to one single factor. He said that throughout the course he had relived one experience after another throughout his career recalling exactly how he had lost sales. And each time he marvelled at how the techniques had been documented in such simple language. "But there seems to be no second chance in selling," he continued, "when you lose one, it's usually lost forever." He was good at analyzing situations as well as himself. He was a little late, though, a mistake too many salesmen make.

Don't be late. Don't catch up at the end of your business career. Start doing it now and reap the profits. Force yourself to become analytical. Ask yourself the question "why" over and over again each day. Speculate constantly as to why somebody did something. Why they did it a certain way. Try to come up with answers that are reasonable, that fit the situation. Such exercises train your mind to become analytical. The more such self training you do—the sharper you become.

Analyze carefully the advertising campaigns of successful products. You will find that they invariably follow the *golden formula of super salesmanship*. This is a formula you should know and never forget. It should guide you in every single sales situation you encounter. Here's the formula:

1.  Intrigue the interest of your prospect.
2.  Create a state of suspense in his mind.
3.  Make your presentation.
4.  Close with an urge for the desired action.

### Checking up on yourself

*Analysis* and *check up* seem to go hand in hand. By check up we mean the periodic instances when a salesman takes a hard look at himself as to where he's been, how he's doing and where he's headed. If you become analysis conscious, you begin to ask many questions of yourself —a very healthy situation in sales work.

A few years ago we were conducting one of our demonstration sessions of the Jack Lacy Course in Providence, Rhode Island. These sessions are always open to the public. All interested parties are invited to attend without obligation. Those who decide to take the course sign up. The others will have gained some knowledge without paying a penny. It's a fun night. There's always a little hoopla, a few stories, a film and, of course, some sales training techniques. A very good friend of mine in the insurance business lived in that area so I invited him to attend. He was delighted. He didn't miss a trick. He took in every single word and got a big charge out of the humorous stories. At the end of the evening he told me how much he had enjoyed himself but didn't take too much of my time so I could be free to talk to the prospects for the course.

Months later I was with him socially and the subject of the course and the demonstration session he had attended came up. I was amazed at the single thing that had impressed him most. "The man in the canoe." At first I didn't quite know what he meant. But as he described his reactions, it then became quite clear. The film we show during that session is entitled, "Mr. Organizer and the Hot Button." About halfway through the film a man with a blank expression on his face is shown sitting in a canoe, not bothering to paddle, and headed for a suicidal waterfall. The audio portion of the film makes the point that this man is *drifting*. My friend never forgot that. He had related strongly. He had decided that he was drifting and that his sales were down for that reason. It sparked him. He made the turn and not too long after that he was promoted to district sales manager.

It's easy to drift. Particulary in selling, if with little effort you happen to have a very good month or a very good year, it's a simple matter to begin to "take it easy." So simple that it almost comes naturally. And when this drifting stage comes about, it may last for such a long period of time that the injurious effects may leave a permanent scar. A drifting salesman defies the laws of nature and you can't do that without paying the penalty. One of nature's most positive laws is, "Grow or die." Think about it. It makes a great deal of sense. The minute you stop growing you begin to die. There just doesn't seem to be an intermediate status. So when the salesman begins to drift, he's not just standing still, he has begun to die.

We've seen hundreds of cases of drifting—salesmen

who have been sent to our sales course because their companies detected that they needed to be salvaged. Do you think these men will admit that they are in a drifting stage? Never. They rationalize masterfully. Like the stagnating beginner in Chapter one, they blame the economy, the territory, the product line, home office politics, problems at home, saturation of the market, and many other factors. They have excuses galore—it's never laziness or boredom. On the very rare occasions when a salesman will admit that he has sort of "slowed down" he quickly adds that he did it intentionally and then comes a whole new and different set of rationalizations. How many meals can you eat in one day? How many suits of clothes can you wear at one time? How many cars can you drive? Why do you need a lot of money when your children are grown, married and on their own?

No matter which of these categories these men fall into, we know they're in trouble. For a variety of reasons, they have reached a point in their sales careers where the will to fight for every possible order is no longer strong. It's an attitudinal problem, without question, and it's not easy to overcome it. But, more often than not, we do. And without directly referring to it. The course itself becomes *check-up time*. By reviewing the various selling techniques these men begin to realize how much of a rut they have been in. They think about their sales presentations of the recent past and realize how poorly they have been performing on sales calls. An awakening takes place. Towards the end of the course, when they make a presentation to the rest of the class on the product or service which they sell, it all becomes perfectly clear. The presentation which they prepare for the class in no way resembles the presentation they have been making to the real prospect out in the field. It happens automatically and yet subliminally. But the important thing is that it happens. They leave rejuvenated and inspired. They're ready to conquer new horizons. Strange thing, though. How few of these individuals ever say anything which admits guilt. That egotism we've been talking about comes into play. But it doesn't matter. As soon as the drifting has been checked the man has been salvaged.

It is tragic but true that of all the men who pursue a selling career, 75 percent of them are financially insecure at the age of 65. After years of selling they are struggling along at retirement age and greatly dependent upon social security checks. Unbelievable, isn't it? Generation after generation this very same figure keeps turning up. In a profession noted for its high income level one would think that upon retirement the nest egg would be substantial. But it doesn't work out that way. The pattern is a well-established one. In the beginning, the young salesman fights like a panther for every order he gets. He is fighting for survival—striving to insure for himself a permanent job with his company. He has a wife, a mortgage, a baby, car payments and a host of other reasons why he must fight from morning till night and never let up. But then he reaches a point in life when the mortgage payment is no longer a chief worry. The children have finished college and are on their own. He's spending more time at the golf course or on his boat than he ever did before. At this turning point his sales productivity curve flattens out. From then on he can be labelled a drifter. His productivity begins to show a slow but steady downward trend. By the time he reaches retirement age he has dipped substantially into his savings and ends up with very little to show for his many years of high income.

Oh, I can hear exactly what you're saying: "It won't

be me." That's easier said than done. But don't misunderstand. I'm not trying to throw gloom your way. I'm merely pointing out that, in selling, you can determine your own destiny. These horrible things won't happen to you *only if* you develop and maintain the determination to succeed by constantly growing and never letting up. How do you do this? To do your best work constantly you need incentives to spur you on. Incentives bring about your greatest effort. If someone supplies them for you in the form of a promised promotion, or increased income, or sales contests, bonuses or prizes—you're in good shape. But since you should never depend on what someone else will provide for you, you should also develop incentives of your own. It is very easy to do this. Decide on certain goals for yourself and then work towards them. If you want a better house in a nicer neighborhood, make the new house your goal. Drive by the ritzy part of town once a week. That helps you to keep the goal before you. Take a small piece of adhesive tape and place it on the dashboard of your car. Write the letter "H" on it. Only you will know what it stands for,— your new *house*. But every time you get in and out of your car it will remind you to work harder towards your goal. When you finally move into the better house, set up another goal and work towards it.

Some will argue that a goal may be dangerous to one's morale. If you set one up and don't attain it, the disappointment is hard to overcome. Nonsense. Better to have an overly-ambitious goal than to have none at all. Companies in all fields of industry are known to establish sales quotas that are almost beyond reach. But in the process they end up with substantial sales increases. And interestingly enough, those members of the sales force who complain bitterly when quotas are announced invariably fail to attain them. The professional salesmen who take quotas in stride, on the other hand, usually meet them or, with pride, exceed them. With the latter it's a challenge. Everything with them is a challenge. That's why they are so successful.

Not all salesmen become sales managers, for a number of reasons. No need to discuss all of these reasons here, save for the one that relates to the subject at hand. Strange as it may seem, many salesmen don't make it because to become a sales manager was never a goal. You have to want something and work towards it in order to get it.

Jim Jackson took the Lacy Course eight years ago. At about the halfway mark he phoned me one morning and asked if we could have lunch together. We did and I was duly impressed. Here was a young man, 24 years old, who knew exactly where he wanted to go. In class it had been obvious that he possessed a marvelous sales personality but what really made him tick hadn't come out in the open. It did at the restaurant. He had a plan. A well laid-out plan for his future. It called for a promotion every two years. He had it down on paper. It looked like this:

| Years | Position |
|---|---|
| 1 & 2 | Salesman |
| 3 & 4 | Assistant Dist. Sales Manager |
| 5 & 6 | District Sales Manager |
| 7 & 8 | National Sales Manager |
| 9 & 10 | Vice President |
| 11 & on | President |

He was proud of his plan and as confident as is humanly possible. He asked for my opinion and I commended him enthusiastically. He smiled and said,—"I knew you'd approve. Not everyone does. My own wife thinks I'm crazy. She thinks I ought to let success just happen and not push. But I've got to know where I'm going. I must set goals and proceed to meet them." I agreed. We talked a while about his approaches, all based on curiosity, and then we parted.

Two years later, almost to the day, he was on the phone again. "You may congratulate me, if you wish," said he, "for you are now speaking with the newly appointed *assistant district sales manager,*—who was promoted right on schedule." I congratulated him and we chatted. His voice bubbled over like freshly-opened champagne. And why not? He had proved something to himself. At the end of our conversation, instead of "goodbye" he said, "Call you in two years."

And that he did. Only this time it was a personal visit. Not quite as bubbly, I noticed, but there was a reason. As the new *district sales manager,* he had brought one of his salesmen with him, to enroll him in the Lacy Course, and he played the role of a management official in a most dignified manner.

The next visit came at about eighteen months later. Jim called while I was out of the office and obtained an appointment. This time things were different. He was serious and rather concerned. The sales manager in his company had been told to find himself another job and Jim had asked his vice president for a promotion into that position. "He laughed," said Jim "and I was furious. He told me that this was an important job requiring much more experience than I have. Whatever I said he ridiculed. When I told him about my goals his belly laugh could be heard throughout the sales department. And then he gave me the final crusher. He said that perhaps I had been brought along much too fast and, most likely, that's why my head is so big."

I asked Jim if he had lost confidence in the management of his company to the degree that he would want to leave. He said, "Most decidedly and I've already found another job. I'm here to discuss it with you." We did and he had all the possible facts upon which to base a decision. What interested me particularly was the youth and aggressiveness of top management. I agreed that the change would be good for him. (I've learned from experience that once you lose confidence in your boss it's time for a change. The damage is usually irreparable.)

As *national sales manager* of his new company Jim had a ball. He was given full responsibility with a free hand to do whatever was necessary to build the sales force and increase sales. I would learn of his continued progress through the salesmen he sent to our courses, all of whom had nothing but praise for him. One of them, a young lady, referred to her boss as a "tiger you can love."

Four months ago Jim wrote me a very nice letter. In it he thanked me for my interest in him and then went on to extoll the virtues of the Jack Lacy Course and the instructors at the Institute. The title under his signature? *Vice President.*

At the age of 32 Jim holds an important job at top-management level. It didn't just happen. He planned it that way. There's nothing supernatural about him. He's a normal, red-blooded male with an average intellect. His schedule calls for him to become president of his company in about two years. At 34? I wouldn't bet against him.

You may say, "Well, so that's one isolated case. Anyone can single out the exception to the rule." True—but that's not the case here. With human beings there can be an army of exceptions. It all depends on the individuals and their attitudes.

Jim Jackson decided early in life to set goals for his future and to have check points along the way to insure his progress. You can do likewise and for this it's never too late. Following the sales techniques within these pages will automatically raise you high above the masses. The rest is up to you. How far you eventually go and what heights you attain will be determined by you and you alone.

Like Jim, you can grow very rapidly if you want to and if you apply yourself. Stick-to-it-iveness is more than half the battle, no matter what the goals may be.

There must be hundreds of people with my background who could have written this book—if they wanted to. Some probably thought about it many times. Years from now they'll still be thinking about it.

Leave them *all* behind. Start *doing* NOW.